MW00937109

Confessions of a Greaser

By:

Bobby Darrell White

Bobby Darrell White

ISBN-13: 978-1502361134
ISBN-10: 1502361132

About the Author

Bobby Darrell White is a retired Accounting and Financial executive who has worked in the broadcast, entertainment, television production, and not-for-profit industries. He has published many technical articles on Finance and Accounting, and has written guest columns for various newspapers. He currently lives in Green Township, Ohio, a suburb of Cincinnati.

White earned his Bachelor's Degree in Accounting at Thomas More College and has, in addition, studied Finance, Business Law, and Public Relations.

Bobby Darrell White

Acknowledgments

No book could be written without support
and encouragement.   Thanks to my wife
Joyce, my daughter Nickie and her husband
David, and my son Rob and his wife Trish for
their part in encouraging me to work at my
passion of writing.

Credit should also go to all of my friends who
read my books before they are published.
They are my staunchest critics, and I thank
them for their advice.

Disclaimers

The characters depicted in this book are real but their names have been changed to protect their anonymity, except the names of my immediate family, relatives, and the names of established businesses in Cumberland that exists, or have existed, during the late 1940s up to, and including, 1961.

Any resemblance to fictional names given to the persons mentioned above in this book to real persons, living or deceased, is purely coincidental.

All the products mentioned in this book are protected by trademarks.

Table of Contents

Chapter 1

"How old would you be if you didn't know how old you were"?
Satchel Paige

I t was August, 1955 when I started the seventh grade. The buildings that housed Cumberland, Kentucky's Junior High School, unlike the two-story red brick structure of the elementary school that I attended, were wooden. Although the buildings were located on the same property, situated on a hill overlooking Cumberland High School, the differences were noticeable. The wooden buildings were old, smelly, and unattractive, but we seventh graders felt special to have been separated from the elementary school into our own space. Those same wooden buildings once housed the first through sixth grades, and the brick structure that was the elementary school once housed grades seven through twelve. A new high school was built a short distance away and was dedicated in 1949.

The teachers in Junior High were not really prepared for us at that time. Our ages were twelve and thirteen years old with

7

raging hormones that would have made Casanova and Fanny Hill envious. We were the kings and queens of "cool" and we emulated James Dean and Natalie Wood who starred in the 1955 movie "Rebel without a Cause," which is still considered one of the greatest cult movies of all time. The name rebel, taken from the context of that movie, was given to us to describe our new and changing views of school and the world. To us, school was not only a place to learn, it was also the primary place for meeting and bantering with the opposite sex, our haven from the world of "square" adults and authority figures, and a place to practice our heads-up swagger. The world outside of Cumberland, Kentucky, to us, was as far as the moon and even non-existent to some.

Figure 1. James Dean. "Rebel without a Cause."

In 1955, Bill Haley and the Comets recorded "Rock Around the Clock," and an unknown singer from Memphis recorded his first hit song, "I Forgot to Remember to Forget," that soared to number one on the COUNTRY charts. His name was Elvis Presley. This new music, which later was to be called Rock and Roll, a term that Alan Freed, a DJ from Cleveland, Ohio, borrowed from the lexicon of the South where the name Rock and Roll had an entirely different meaning; in the south, youngsters used the phrase as a reference to dancing and sexual intercourse, but luckily the meaning of the term was masked well from the censors of the day or that music genre may have been named "Yelling and Screaming," (or a similar term) which would have been more appropriate to confused parents, churches, and "social police."

Pop culture, especially in the mid-1950s, was exploding. Teenagers were driving their parents crazy with their new music, hot rods, hair styles, dance moves, dress, and the use of terms such as "man" as in the following conversation:

"Hey, man, did you see that chick's headlights."

"Yeah, man, she is really cool. I would love to see that double slingshot that she is wearing to hold up those things. I would bet that the straps are straining from the weight and loving it."

"Yeah, man, I know what you mean."

"Hey, man, do you want to go the drive-in tonight."

"No, man, I don't have the bread. I'm tapped out."

Parents, of course, were worried that their Bobby Darrell's and Peggy Sue's were losing their language skills and their futures were, to them, looking dim.

"How could anyone ever get a job talking such gobbledygook and dressing the way that you do," they would say. "And your father and I are worried that you are going to go deaf and crazy listening to that stupid Rock and Roll music. And who is that Elvis guy, anyway. What an odd name to give to a child. He won't go far in life with that name, hair, and his pink shirts. He looks like a juvenile delinquent and should be arrested for the bad influence that he is having on the kids in this country. And that Carl Perkins guy singing 'Blue Suede Shoes!' What boy or man would wear blue shoes anyway? He would be the laughing stock of the whole town.....etc."

The further fear of the direction of our generation was amplified with the release in 1954 of the movie "The Wild One" starring Marlon Brando and Lee Marvin, the story of two rival motorcycle gangs who terrorized a town in California. Many teens bought the same type of black leather motorcycle jacket that Brando wore in the movie and copied his every move. Parents gasped at the number of black leather jackets being worn by their sons and they thought that the world was being overrun by juvenile delinquents and hardened criminals.

Figure 2. Marlon Brando as "The Wild One."

As advocates for the new popular culture, we guys dove in headfirst into what we thought was proper behavior of the day for teenagers. We wanted our hair styled to look exactly like Elvis', and to get the sheen of his hair, we piled on the Brylcream despite the manufacturers claim that "a little dab'll do ya." We bought combs and kept them in our front shirt pockets so that we could be prepared at any time to comb back any errant hairs, and we chewed gum incessantly because it was the thing to do. We wore tight jeans with the cuffs rolled up, shoes or boots with a buckle across the front instead of laces, wide leather belts similar to the one worn by Brando in "The Wild One," and sunglasses that looked identical to Brando's. We were a sight to behold, and minister's Sunday morning sermons were directed at us young "misfits," admonishing us for our wicked ways. They also appealed to us to adhere to the dress code established by adults so that we would look like humans again, all the more reason to dress the way that we did because we enjoyed the term "rebel."

The girls wore many different hair styles, but would not even think of straight hair; it was always curled, or styled with waves. There was a Liz Taylor look, a Marilyn Monroe look, many varieties of pony tails, long wavy hair, and numerous short hair styles. At the malt shop, the poodle skirt with a petticoat and a sweater top was popular but any dress or skirt worn, regardless of style, was usually well below the knees. Girls typically dressed far more conservatively than the boys, and they had a much wider selection of fashions.

Being popular was more important to the girls than the boys, and the way to become more popular was to walk arm in arm with the most popular of the boys and be as stylish as possible while throwing glances at the other girls that said "look at me." They wore make-up to cover their pimples and zits, sometimes so thick that we guys thought that it had to be scraped off at night.

The 1950s was the first decade that young people from the ages of thirteen through nineteen were called teenagers, a label that was used and misused by the media for various reasons, and in advertising to describe and influence that age group. Depending on the source, the teen years were vicariously described as "that awkward" age, the "tween years," (or a transition period between childhood and adulthood), the "difficult years," the age of "rebellion," and some even labeled us as the "lost" generation.   But we looked at ourselves as a generation that was much different than our parents were at that age. The world was changing rapidly, and we viewed our parents as "old fashioned," "square," and not "with it" when confronting new challenges.   Without knowing it, we were to become the future inventors of the personal computer, the internet, cell phones, 3D television sets, and other technologies that futurists before us could only dream about. We would become the captains of our own destinies and shock the world with our boldness and fearlessness when challenged with new and complex problems.

In the mid-1950s, the car culture exploded. Cruising through town became a favorite activity with young teens who, fortunately, had a father and mother that trusted them with the family car. Being seen, especially by the girls, driving through town in our dad's "land yacht" was a thrill. Attendance at the drive-in theater was becoming more popular, and it was packed on Friday and Saturday nights. The movies were not important, it was finding a spot as far from the screen as we could possibly get; the back row was an ideal place for our tête-à-têtes. We would turn on the radio and listen to the music of the day and stare at each other and the night sky while avoiding the movie altogether. Shyness was not one of our traits when we were at the drive-in; the back seat was a favorite place to sit and "watch" a movie and neck. After "watching" movies until the drive-in closed, we rushed to get our Peggy Sue's home to angry parents if we were only 15 minutes past their curfew.

Our days were spent, both in and out of school, concentrating not on our future, but on making plans for next week-end's activities. While we worked hard in school to obtain good grades, which was important to us, there was a lot of time for recreation in between. Most of us loved school, but we also loved our freedom to do what greasers and greaserettes do – enjoy and celebrate life in our own way.

Chapter 2

"Beauty, unaccompanied by virtue, is as a flower without perfume."
Proverb

Seventh grade was, for most of us, much more difficult than the sixth. Concentrating on school work and attempting to free the mind of distractions, which were everywhere, was next to impossible. We changed our vocabulary relating to ourselves and to school in general. We were no longer boys and girls; we were teens, and everyone was corrected when they used the term boy or girl, and among us greasers the word for school became the "institution."

Our teacher was Sandra Donovan, a nice looking lady in her mid-twenties. She was somewhat overweight and had the looks of a beauty in a painting from the renaissance when ladies of her heft were considered ideal beauties. She had bottled blond hair with roots that appeared to be dark brown or black. Her eyes were brown and her eyelids were always meticulously made up with far too much eye shadow. Her skin was smooth and well-tanned, and it looked as though she had spent a lot of time either on the beach or sunning by the pool at Swimland in Cumberland. She had the largest breasts that I had ever seen on a woman in Cumberland, and she was apparently proud of them; she walked in an upright position with her chest pushed forward as far as she could possibly get it to display what us greasers called her "treasures." There were fantasies discussed among us about going "treasure" hunting and the mother lode that we might discover there. We would later discover that there were many "treasure hunters" in Cumberland who actually did find the mother lode by giving up a different kind of treasure to compensate her for the honor of allowing them to do so.

The fashion of the day for the ladies in the mid-1950s were dresses or skirts that that extended well below the knee. While Miss Donovan's wardrobe complied with the dress code, she would always (purposely, we thought) manage to have her dress to rise above the knee and sometimes to the thigh when crossing her legs exciting us males almost to the point of madness. We never saw women's legs above knee level except in the movies and at the community swimming pool, so we strained our necks trying to catch a peek whenever we could. Being stylish had its rewards and drawbacks as I was later to discover with a simple pair of shoes.

Everyone wanted to have their own style in the 1950s, but I went further in my personal pursuit of it. I, and many others, dressed like James Dean and the girls wanted to look like Natalie Wood, but I was unhappy with the shoe

Figure 3. Natalie Wood.

styles of the day, so I was determined to have a pair that was not manufactured for the masses.

Carl Perkins wrote and recorded a song in 1955 called "Blue Suede Shoes," so every teen male who thought that the shoes were cool hurried out to buy a pair, but I did not want shoes that were becoming overly popular and common among teenage boys.

After giving it much thought, I went shopping at the 5¢ and 10¢ store (better known as the five and dime) and searched for something to color my shoes. Black, brown, oxblood, and now blue swede somehow did not fit my idea of different. After searching for some time, I spotted a small container of the most beautiful gold paint in the hobby section of the store and immediately decided on that color for my soon-to-be stylish shoes.

I hurried home, anxious to become the envy of my friends and classmates by showing off my new shoes. My dad had many sizes of paint brushes, so I found one of the appropriate size and, very carefully, covered the shoes with two coats of the liquid gold, set them outside, and waited impatiently for them to dry. I waited for two hours or so and I marveled at how the paint job turned out. The shoes glittered brightly and I knew instantly that I was as different as one could get when it came to style.

The next day was Saturday. I spent a couple of hours in the afternoon preparing for a stroll through town with three of my friends, something that we did every Saturday afternoon and evening.

"Cool shoes," said Charley Black.

"Yeah, man," said Roger Sherwood, "they are getting a lot of attention from everyone in town. Great idea! Maybe I will paint mine, too, but I am thinking more of a bright red color."

"Have you gone nuts, Roger?" said Manfred Molina, better known as Manny. "Red shoes are for girls. My sister has a pair."

"Are you calling me a girl?" said Roger. "The color red is not for girls only. Your dad drives a red Chevy, doesn't he? Does that make him a girl?"

"Are you calling my dad a girl?" said Manny.

"Hey! Let's not argue about colors and concentrate on impressing the girls," I said. "There are some at the Big Top Drive-In. Let's go there."

We walked normally for about four blocks, and the closer that we got to the Big Top, our walk was slowly becoming a shuffle, and when we were close enough for everyone to see us, the shuffle became a strut. My shoes got everyone's attention, and I was proud of my creation. I made them as visible as I possibly could by placing my hands in my pockets and lifting the pants legs enough to show them off.

Later that evening, when I walked home, the headlights from passing cars heightened the brightness of my shoes, so much so that many drivers said that they could not see me, only my shoes, and they appeared as though they were electrified. The soles, in particular, put on a light show as I strutted on my way home.

When I was ready to discard the shoes after a few weeks of use my friend, Johnny Richter, asked for them. They were too small for him; he suffered great pain in his feet while wearing them to garner the attention that I had received from them.

Johnny made a few visits to the Podiatrist over the following few weeks for foot problems that his parents said mysteriously appeared. The doctor never could diagnose the problem to the satisfaction of his dad and mom.

Whatever happened to the shoes after that is unknown.

Our first class in the seventh grade was Health and Hygiene. The boys became immediately attentive when Miss Donovan asked us to open our health books. In anticipation of learning anatomy from an anatomically blessed teacher, ears and eyes were open to every word that she said. We expected her to point to various parts of her body while explaining its form and function, but we were disappointed to see cartoonish drawings in the book which she referred to instead. Anatomy at that level of school was uninteresting and boring, so we continued to watch every move of HER anatomy hoping for a wardrobe malfunction.

Miss Donovan, despite the distraction that she was to us guys, was a

23

competent teacher, and she seemed to enjoy her job. She loved history and the social sciences; my interests were in the natural and physical sciences and math. I previously had no interest in the subjects that she loved, but her lectures drew my attention to them, which was indicative of her competency. Or was it her physique?

Seventh grade was a fun year for most of us, and I had to thank Miss Donovan for my new found interest on subjects that I previously disliked which made seventh grade far more fun.

In the seventh grade, I frequently had conversations with Diana Smith, who I had a crush on since the fifth grade. She was of perfect proportions (in my eyes), a head shorter than I was, she was enthusiastic about everything that we talked about, and her interests were identical to mine. Her dark blonde hair was shoulder length, and her eyes were bright and a dark blue. She wore very little make-up, except for a light application of lipstick. She was well liked, and everyone enjoyed being around her. She invited me to her house one evening and

24

we did not want to part from each other, but her dad ended our conversation when the hour got a little too late for him. As I walked home that evening, I was convinced that soon she would be my girlfriend.

Diana wanted me to come and see her so often that her parents protested my frequent visits; in order to continue seeing each other, she told them that I was there to help her with her studies. It worked – for a while.

Chapter 3

"A man in love mistakes a pimple for a dimple."
Japanese Proverb

It was the summer of 1956, and we were just beginning our well-deserved vacation from school. In May of that year, I turned fourteen years old and I felt on top of the world. Diana helped me celebrate by inviting me to a party at her house.

When I arrived, I was surprised at the number of her friends and acquaintances that showed up. Not having much to do except play records and dance (an activity that was not within the purview of my talents), we had to create some type of entertainment to keep everyone busy and happy. The time-tested game of Post Office was our first attempt at entertainment and it was a big success.

Post Office (the kissing game) was always a favorite game of mine at a party. It gave me and everyone else present the opportunity to kiss many members of the opposite sex and enjoy the nuances of the many ways of kissing. At this particular party, though, Marci Canova would always call my number when it was her turn to do so.

Marci was short, with shoulder length auburn hair, and looked a lot younger than fourteen years old. Her lips were full and she used them enthusiastically in her kissing. When I was called into the room, which was darkened considerably for the game, she would put her arms around me and kiss me as passionately as Diana would. She would also keep me in the room beyond our allotted time, as indicated by yells of "Pony Express" by those impatient for the game to continue. "Pony Express" was a term used when suspicions arose that participants in the darkened room were "horsing around." I sensed that Diana did not like it when Marci called my number every time and the amount of time that we spent kissing. I was sure that she would approach me about it after the party was over.

In the year of 1956, the average salary was $4,450, a new house sold for an average of $11,700 (to rent one would have cost $88 per month), the inflation rate was only 1.52%, a new car cost $2,050 and gasoline sold for 22¢ a gallon. Elvis recorded his first #1 popular hit "Heartbreak Hotel," written by Mae Axton, a lady that I would later meet and chat with while working for Multimedia Entertainment. He also recorded "Hound Dog" and "Don't Be Cruel" that same year.

If popular culture exploded in 1955, it went nuclear in 1956. Changes came quickly, and it was becoming difficult for most of us to keep up with the latest technology. IBM invented the computer hard drive with a whopping 5 MB of storage space, the first commercial VCR went on sale, and the first Transatlantic Telephone Cable went into operation. A major breakthrough in the medical field occurred when Dr. Albert Sabin of Cincinnati's Children's Hospital developed an oral vaccine for polio.

There were many things to do in Cumberland in the mid-1950s. We had two popular restaurants, the Big Top and Pine View, where most all of the greasers and greaserettes would flock to every Saturday night. Those were the places where we could showcase our "coolness" and our latest girlfriends at the time.

We also had the Auburn Drive-In Theater just outside of Cumberland. My close circle of friends were too young to drive; some of us would double-date with the ones who could with the requirement that we pay the admission price for the driver's date, a small price to pay for an evening of bliss. It was a general rule, though, that the driver and his date would occupy the back seat of the car once we were parked. It was easy for them to slump below the rear-view mirror so that the front seat occupants could not see what they were doing, a fine place to be for serious necking sessions. The couple occupying the front seats had to use a little more discretion in their pursuit of lovemaking. Diana and I were fortunate to have found a couple, Richard and Linda, who we double dated with on our first evening at the Auburn.

The main feature of the evening was "Bella Lugosi Meets a Brooklyn Gorilla," a silly movie starring Bella Lugosi, who also starred in the original "Dracula" movie. Lugosi was such a success in "Dracula" that the studios used his fame to film some of the worst movies ever made. It was a comedy, horror, and science fiction movie all in one. If you did not like the comedy, then maybe you would like the horror or science fiction part of the movie. Of course at that time, no one cared for Lugosi movies, so they were ideal to show at a Drive-In venue.

Once the movie started, all lights around the outside of the concession stand area were dimmed. That was our signal to raise our windows. Already, our hot breath and body heat were steaming them up, and all sorts of sounds could be heard coming from the cars around us:

"Keep your hands high and wide, Romeo, or you can take me home," said Audrey from a car close by.

"If you do that one more time, I'll pull your fingernails out, you pervert," said Sue from another car.

"Proceed with caution, Billy, and you know what I mean!" said Bonnie from yet another car. "If you want to play, you must bring the toys with you."

A couple must have been playing a familiar game in some unseen car; the girl kept yelling "bingo, bingo, bingo." If I were that bored, I think that I would have stayed home and played Monopoly.

Figure 4. At the Drive-In.

After the first movie, it was intermission time, and crowds of teens with rumpled clothes and mussed up hair proceeded to the concession stand hurriedly. I took a comb that I kept at all times in my shirt pocket and combed back my hair, as I did many times per day to look presentable. Diana did the same, but with her own comb. She had told me many times before that she did not want to use my comb because it always had too much Brylcream in it.

31

We met many friends and acquaintances at the concession stand, and they were saying how great the movie was and how much they were enjoying it. When asked what part of it that they liked best, the topic changed quickly. Many of them did not even know the title of the movie just shown. We all hurriedly exchanged pleasantries and went back to our "necking nest," as the back row of the Drive-In was dubbed.

At the conclusion of the movie, we frantically cleaned the moisture from the glass. We drove away with a smile on our faces and a warm feeling for our dates.

When we arrived at Diana's house, she asked me to join her on the front porch swing. We had time left before her curfew ended to talk. It was almost midnight, and the air was so cool that we cuddled close to each other. I was beginning to like her for her enthusiasm and conversation. We were growing closer each time that we met, and I was going to have a hard time leaving her for the evening.

"I really enjoyed our evening together," I said. "I look forward to going to the Auburn Drive-In with you again soon. Richard and Linda also seemed to have had a good time."

"Yes, they did. Did you know what they were doing back there?"

"To be honest with you, no, I didn't. There seemed to be a lot of movement back there. I can only imagine what they were doing."

"You must not have done it before."

"Done what?" I replied with a puzzled look.

"IT! You know, IT," she said with a smile on her face.

"Oh! Now I know what you mean. Really? With us in the car? That took some nerve."

"Have you ever done IT?" she asked with a wide smile.

"It depends on what "IT" is," I said. I was puzzled as to why she was asking me the question.

"Come here and kiss me," she said.

As I was kissing her, she took my hand and placed it on her breast. At first I was shocked at her bold move. She squeezed my hand that was on her breast.

"Do you like that? I do."

"I....I....do, too," I said nervously.

We continued this for about ten minutes, and I was becoming breathless from the excitement. We were so distracted that we did not hear her dad call her name. We heard the door open, and we quickly assumed a position where only my arm around her shoulder could be seen in the darkness.

"Time to come in, Diana," he said harshly. "You have five minutes."

I arose to leave, and as I did, she pulled me closely and hugged me tightly. Our bodies were in full contact, and she gave me a long kiss that seemed to last only seconds. Those five minutes passed in what appeared to be only an instant.

"Sorry, I must go," she said. "We will get together next week - maybe. It depends on the mood of my parents. They do not mind me seeing you, but they have a rule: three evenings a week, and that is it. Would you like to see me Monday or Tuesday evening?"

"Monday," I said quickly.

Chapter 4

"The body is a house of many windows."
Robert Louis Stevenson

Rock and Roll music had its roots prior to 1956, but 1956 was the year that was the genesis of the revolution in that genre.

Elvis Presley recorded "Hound Dog" with "Don't be Cruel" on the flip side. As soon as I had enough money, I went to Keller Music in Cumberland and bought the recording, a 78 rpm version, which was the only one that was compatible with our record player at home, and I played both songs over and over. At Swimland, our pool that was open to the public for a small charge, the recording was played almost continuously on both sides.

The Billboard chart's top 100 songs of 1956 was packed with Rock music. Other than Elvis, Bill Haley and the Comets, Carl Perkins, Fats Domino, Gene Vincent, Little Richard, Chuck Berry, and many other teen idols were scorching the airwaves with music that teenagers wanted to dance to. The various record labels were pressing vinyl records overtime to meet the demands for this new music, and concert venues were always sold out that featured the new stars. Fan magazines were enjoying skyrocketing sales when young rock stars were featured on their covers, and endorsements from anyone who had a current Rock and Roll hit were selling everything from record players, to lunch boxes and numerous toys.

It was, at this time, that I thought that I was ready to make a contribution to this new music by buying a guitar and learning everything that I could about the instrument. I did find one that I bought at a bargain, and I called on my double first cousin, Virgie Creech, to teach me how to play. She was a competent guitar player and a good singer, so I made a great choice for an instructor.

The first chords that that she taught me were G, D, and A. Later, I would learn the chords E, B, C and F. With those chords, I could play almost all of the songs that were on Billboard's top 100 chart by using major chords, or I thought that I could. Virgie guided my left hand over the various strings to form chords and she said to practice, practice, practice until callouses formed on the ends of my fingers and, most importantly, learn to chord the guitar without looking down at it. After many days and nights of practice, I was able to competently chord and change chords quickly without looking down at the guitar.

The first song that I learned on the guitar was Elvis' "That's All Right" and I played it in the chord of E. I sang the song as I played and I felt comfortable at what I was doing.

Figure 5. Virgie Creech.

Virgie was proud of my accomplishments, but she said that the song would probably sound better in C. She did not seem too excited about my singing either, which I could not understand. I later found out, by listening to a taped recording of my singing and playing, that my skills at rhythm guitar was competent enough for the song, but my dreams of a career as a Rock and Roll singer sadly ended that day for me.

I was not the only one who suddenly had an interest in music. Many parents, at the request of their sons and daughters, started buying guitars, drums, pianos, and brass instruments for their future musicians. Parents thought that the instruments might someday be used to play in a symphony orchestra or in one of the big bands such as, Duke Ellington's or Tommy Dorsey's. They never suspected that Rock and Roll music was the only interest that they had. Most of them, like me, finally realized that music was not for them and they looked to other careers that would be more compatible with their natural abilities.

I saw Diana almost every day without her parents ever knowing that we were seeing each other so frequently. I loved to talk to her; she was so intelligent and engaging. My friend Manny said that Diana and I were like a pair of gloves; one was no good without the other.

"Manny, coming from you, that is a

Figure 6. Socrates.

deep philosophical statement. You are Cumberland's answer to Socrates," I said.

"Who is Socrates?" asked Manny.

Now I had some explaining to do, I thought.

"Socrates is that fellow who Plato wrote about."

"Who is Plato?" asked Manny.

"Let me put it this way, Manny, Socrates and Plato were two smart cool cats who lived in Greece over 2,400 years ago. They were Philosophers."

"Oh! Why didn't you say that before?" said Manny. "I don't care about Philosophy or two old cats who lived over 2,400 years ago. I can't get my head around 100 years, so how am I able to think about 2,400 years ago? I care for what is happening now, man. Rock and Roll and babes."

It was close to 90° one summer day in 1956 as Diana and I walked to downtown Cumberland to window shop. The sun was intense as it heated the sidewalk; the heat could be felt through our shoes, slowing our pace to almost a crawl. The perspiration poured from our faces and we immediately sought relief.

"Let's walk over to the park and sit under the shelter," Diana said. "I cannot stand to be out in this heat. I feel like I am being fried."

We stopped at a nearby gas station and bought a couple of ice cold RC Colas, and sat under the park shelter and drank them in just a few gulps. We were comforted by the cold liquid, but we drank them so quickly that we experienced "brain freeze," a condition that everyone is familiar with who has eaten ice cream too exuberantly.

The park was packed with others trying to find comfort from the heat. Air conditioning was rare in homes at that time in Cumberland; an electric fan or an escape to shady areas in the outdoors was the only relief that one could get from the kind of blistering heat that we experienced that day.

We were sitting in the shelter facing Swimland, which was close by. We watched as some frolicked in the water, some were diving, and some were lying in the sun to improve their tans. I had no desire to swim on a day like that; the sun reflects off the water while swimming which exasperates the dangers of sunburn.

"I do not understand why someone would lie in this hot sun on hot concrete for ANY reason," I said. "I do not believe that I could do it for any length of time."

"I have a tan," said Diana. "I love the sun, but not on a day like this. I get a deep tan every summer."

"Yes, I know. I have noticed how dark your face and arms are. I have to admit, you do look good with a tan."

"It is not just my arms and face, you know."

"Oh, then your legs are tanned, also? You will have to show me sometime."

"You don't understand. It is not only my face, arms, and legs, it is my entire body."

"I would love to see all of your tan."

"I will show you sometime," she said with a smile.

She is just teasing me, I thought. If I could get the opportunity to see all of her tan, what should I say? What should I do? How should I react? Why am I asking myself these questions? If it happens and if I said nothing at all, it would at least be a memory that I would never forget.

School was almost ready to resume in the first part of August and we were getting prepared for the big day. Our parents were busy buying us new clothes, shoes and school supplies. We were well equipped with notebooks, paper, pencils, and all of the necessary tools required of an eighth grader. Eighth grade would not only be our last year of Junior High, it would also be our last year on the "hill."

Chapter 5

"Full nakedness! All my joys are due to thee."
John Donne

We walked into one of the eighth grade classrooms that was to become "home" to about thirty students for the next nine months. There were actually four classrooms that housed about one hundred twenty-five students, the largest number of eighth graders in the history of Cumberland Junior High.

The room was hot, even though it was morning. There were no fans to circulate the air, and the comfort level was worsening. Students were squirming in their seats and wanted to escape the heat in any way possible. Our teacher, Leslie Goodman, made the suggestion that we seek relief by going outside and find a shady spot to study. Although we found an ideal spot, the heat was still too much for most of us.

Leslie Goodman introduced herself on the first day of school as a person who had fun teaching. That was good news for us; most of us had fun learning and it

45

seemed as though we had a person as dedicated to the teaching profession as was our third grade teacher, Betty D., better known to us as Miss Hyde.

Miss Goodman was in her late twenties or early thirties, and was a woman of impeccable tastes in clothing and make-up. She always wore clothes that highlighted her slim figure which was a stunning masterpiece of femininity. Her short, wavy

Figure 7. Audrey Hepburn

hair was a beautiful auburn color that resembled Audrey Hepburn's, a movie star who was always well coiffed in her own unique style which was widely imitated. Her skin was a smooth ivory color that required little or no make-up. Her lips were full; she used just enough red lipstick to highlight her beautiful facial features. Her beauty also attracted the attention of the girls in the class because the guys, especially us greasers, thought that she was the essence of love and sexuality.

46

Once outside, I walked over to Miss Goodman, introduced myself, and told her that I looked forward to the eighth grade. She smiled, thanked me, and said that she was pleased at the fine reception that she received from her students. As she was talking, I could smell her perfume which was obviously expensive and she needed very little of it to be effective. I kept staring at her beautiful face; her teeth were as white as white could possibly get and her eyes drooped just enough to give a mysterious air about her. As she talked, her lips pursed which was the sexiest lip movements that I had ever seen. I was in love with this woman, I thought, and I wanted her to know it.

We stayed outside for just a short period of time when it was announced that school was being dismissed because of the heat; that was the first and only time that I could ever remember heat as a reason to dismiss school. And on our first day of class.

Since we did not have any homework, my friends convinced me to walk to town with them and enjoy the rest of the

47

day. It was only mid-morning and activity in town was low, so there was nothing to do. I was looking for a part-time job to earn a little cash; this was the perfect time to look since proprietors of the businesses in town would have time to talk to me about a job.

The last place that I visited was the Corlee Theater, a favorite place that I had become more than familiar with over the years. I thought that maybe I could get a job working at the concession stand, selling tickets, or even a janitorial job. I talked to the manager briefly and as I did, he asked me if I would consider a job as a projectionist. My eyes opened wide and my jaw dropped at the thought of becoming a projectionist at the Corlee. That meant that I would be able to watch every movie free and it would be a job that I know that I would enjoy.

"I do not know the first thing about running a projector, but I like the idea," I said.

"We will train you," he said. "I have a feeling that you will learn quickly."

He took me upstairs to the projection booth which was above the balcony. Of all the

Figure 8. The Corlee Theater.

years that I attended the Corlee, this was the first time that I had ever been in the balcony. At that time, blacks were not allowed to sit with the white people on the first level because of the shameful Jim Crow laws that existed in the 1950s. The balcony of the Corlee Theater was the only place in Cumberland where they could watch a movie.

I was expecting to see a projector very similar to a home movie projector but in a larger size. The two projectors were much taller than I was and appeared to be harder to learn to operate than I anticipated. The manager asked me to return in the afternoon to begin my training. I was thrilled not only with my new job, but I was to become a key employee at the Corlee.

After a few days of training, I would begin a job that was to last for about three years. Within a short period of time, I also became the projectionist at the Auburn Drive-In in the summer months, which was owned by the same company that managed the Corlee. I would be earning a good income that was above my needs, so I would be able to save some of it for the future.

The next morning, as we entered the classroom, I could not wait to tell everyone about my new job. After congratulations from everyone, Miss Goodman called me aside and personally congratulated me. She put her hand on my shoulder, which sent a feeling that I had never felt before up my back.

"I am so proud that I have a student who has the initiative to work after school at such an important job. Are you going to get me in free sometime?" she quipped.

"Sure," I said. "If I cannot get you in free, I will buy you a ticket."

She giggled and pursed her lips in a way that elevated my heart rate to a probable new high.

After settling in my chair, I kept staring at her for the longest time. She would glance at me often and give me a half smile. All of the guys in the room noticed the attention. I could not imagine what they were going to say at recess.

Other than being one of the most beautiful women that I had ever seen, Miss Goodman was also one of my best teachers. I took notes on everything that she said during her lectures; her tests were a challenge to me, not something to be dreaded.

After school, I wanted to celebrate the acquisition of my new job. It was not my scheduled evening to see Diana, but her parents were leaving for a short trip to her grandmothers who was having health problems. I was, of course, delighted that we were alone and undisturbed.

"Congratulations on your new job," said Diana. "So you will be making a lot of money now, huh?"

"Not as much as one would think. I will be earning more money than I will need for my own personal use, so I plan to save enough to buy a car when I get my driver's license."

"Oh, that would be fun," she said with a wide smile. "I can't wait. Let's go into my bedroom and play some records. I just bought one by the Platters and one by the Diamonds."

Her bedroom was small, but tidy. There was a double bed, a small dresser where she placed her record player, a night stand where her records were neatly stacked, and a small vanity table with a mirror. She had photos of Elvis and Pat Boone over her bed, and photos of movie stars on another wall. I was impressed with her neatness and the way everything was arranged.

"Nice!" I said. "I love your bedroom."

"I will be right back," she said. "I forgot something."

She came back into the room shortly dressed in a robe. I was surprised that she changed her clothes at this early hour.

"I have something to show you," she said.

She stood up, untied the robe, and let it fall to the floor. She was completely naked, and I sat on her bed flabbergasted at her beautiful figure.

"I told you that I was going to show you my tan, remember?"

"Oh, I remember! But I thought that you were kidding."

I looked up and down her body and was amazed at how beautiful she was. As she had said that day in the park, her tan did cover her entire body. Now what do I do, I thought.

Chapter 6

"Sex is an emotion in motion."
Mae West

As she stood there, I was speechless.

"Well how do I look?" she asked. "Do you like the tan?"

"Oh, yes! What is not to like?"

"Have you ever had sex?" she asked, as she sat beside me on the bed.

I was shocked that she would ask me that question. I paused momentarily before answering her.

"No, have you?"

"No, but I have been reading about it."

"You have? What have you been reading?"

"My mom has a book hidden in her closet written by a man named Alfred Kinsey that describes everything."

"Everything? I would love to see it sometime."

"I also believe that my mom teaches other women about sex. She has a group over each month. She has things in the closet for demonstrations while she teaches."

"What kind of things?"

"I'll show you."

She left and returned with a shoe box and opened it. One by one she showed me the contents.

"I don't know why she would demonstrate this," she said as she showed me a rubber penis. "All of those ladies are married, so shouldn't they know what a penis looks like?"

"And this thing! I think that I finally figured it out. It vibrates when I slide this switch. I heard it one evening from my mom's bedroom and I asked her what the sound was. She said it was a muscle relaxer. I tried it on my muscles and all that it did was tickle. It seems useless to me."

"So the ladies gather once a month to talk about sex, huh?"

"Not only that, but my mom gives each one of them a catalog to order this stuff from each month. I believe that they are all teachers and order their supplies from her for demonstrations."

Her eyes opened widely and she gave me a frightened look.

"It's my parents. Leave through the back door as quickly as you can. If they knew that you were here, I would be in a lot of trouble."

I arose from the bed and moved as quickly as I could. I opened the back door and it was so dark that I could not see much of anything. As I started to run I stepped on a cat's tail and it screamed, which frightened me even more.

"Oh, no!" I thought. "I dropped my wallet on the bed or floor. I just hope that her parents don't find it."

I finally made it to the road and quickly picked up my pace. I looked back and much to my relief, I did not see anyone chasing me. So far, so good, I thought. I think that everything is going to be all right now. Or was it?

The next day, Diana brought my wallet with her to school, and said that she could not see me anymore. Her mom discovered it on the bed and she was forced to tell her that I was there. Both her mom and dad were so angry at her that she was forbidden to leave the house indefinitely except to go to and from school. I felt bad that she had gotten into trouble, but there was nothing that I could do to reverse what had happened.

I was so depressed the next day by not being able to speak to Diana that Miss Goodman sensed that something was wrong. She asked me to remain after school to have a chat with her.

"Is there something seriously wrong with you? I have noticed that your attention is not on your work. Is there anything that I can do?"

"No. Diana and I broke up. We were inseparable. It is as if someone close to me died."

"So sorry. May I get personal and ask what caused the breakup? Maybe I could talk to Diana."

"What caused it? Well, it is kind of personal, and I would be too embarrassed to tell you anyway."

"You can tell me. I am your teacher, and it is my job to help whenever I can. Everything that you tell me will remain confidential."

"O.k.," I said.

My face turned red as I described exactly what happened. She looked at me as though she was shocked.

"Did you have sex with Diana?"

"Oh, no! I would not quite call it having sex. We just talked about it."

"Well, I wouldn't worry about it if I were you. Her parents have no reason to blame you for anything. I suppose that it would do no good to talk to Diana. It is not her that is your problem, it is her parents."

"Yes, but it bothers me because I feel responsible for her punishment."

"It is best, then, that you get on with your life. If you need my assistance in any way, please let me know."

"By the way, I am going to the Corlee Theater Saturday afternoon to see 'Anything Goes.' If you are working on that day, I would like to see the projection booth. I have never seen one before."

"Great! I would love to show you around. The best time for a visit would be about forty-five minutes before the movie starts."

"I will be there."

Just the thought of Miss Goodman coming to see the projection booth was so exciting to me that I began to tremble. I would be alone with her and I intended to show her every piece of equipment and how it worked as an excuse to extend the time of her visit for as long as possible.

After the last bell, I went to the Corlee Theater for my final day of training. I felt as though I was already competent enough for the job, but the manager wanted to watch me closely to assure that I did not make any mistakes. He allowed me to work on my own under his watchful eye for a couple of hours after which he gave me the thumbs up and said that tomorrow, a Friday, I would be on my own.

I could not wait to celebrate, but I did not have anyone to celebrate with at this late hour, so I stopped off at Lawrence's Pool Room for a game of nine ball with Robert Nolan., a frequent patron of the establishment.

"Hey, Bobby Darrell," he said. "I heard that you were having girl trouble."

"How did you know?"

"Word gets around fast in Cumberland. I heard that you had sex with Diana and her dad and mom grounded her indefinitely."

"Who told you that?"

"I heard it from her mom's friend, Elsa. She told her everything about it. So is it true?"

"It is not true and I would prefer not to talk about it, Robert. Let's just play a game of pool. I have to leave shortly."

As we continued our game of billiards, I thought about Diana and all the gossip that must be spreading about her among others. I was both hurt and angry that someone like Robert was complicit in further damaging her reputation over something that never happened.

After the first bell on Friday and settling in our seats, Miss Goodman gave us a lecture on the history of mass media and its use as a tool for both good and evil. It was a timely subject, and since I was thinking of what Robert said at the pool hall yesterday, I thought that it was an opportune time to speak up.

"Would it be wrong to say that news and gossip via word of mouth was the first form of mass media?" I asked.

"Tell me more about your thoughts on news and gossip as a form of mass media," she said.

"Well, before the written word, that was the only way to communicate to members of the community in which they lived. If news was spread to the community and beyond by using word of mouth, slow as it might have been, would that not be a form of mass media?"

"In a way, you are right, but in discussing mass media, I was thinking more about newspapers, radio, and television. Word of mouth was a way to get information to the community and it was important, I suppose, at the time."

"I know for a fact that as news spreads by word of mouth, the message is not as accurate as it was when it was first uttered. Would you agree with that?"

"Yes, that is an accurate statement. If you whisper something to a person sitting in front of you, and they whisper the same message to the person in front of them and it continues to the last person in the room, the message to the last person would be very much unlike the original one."

"So if someone gossips about another person and it spreads, say to twenty people, the message would likely be totally inaccurate when told to the twentieth person."

"That is true," she said.

"Then I would like to tell my friends in this room to not rely on the accuracy of any gossip that you hear. It would hurt not only the person that is the subject of gossip, but it could also hurt you someday under the same circumstances."

I think that Miss Goodman knew exactly what I meant. She smiled and nodded her head slightly at me.

Chapter 7

"Grant me chastity and continence, but not yet."
Augustine of Hippo

Roger, Manny, Charley, and I always arrived at school early every morning, as many did, to kibitz with others who also arrived early. The three of them were my best friends throughout my elementary and high school years.

Manny Molina was a second generation Italian-American who towered over all of us; he was well above six feet in height, muscular, and athletic. He was the fourth of six children, as I am, with the gift of understanding anything mechanical. It was said that he could dismantle an automobile completely and reassemble it within a week. He was also a ladies man, although his humor would indicate otherwise. His black wavy hair, dark brown eyes, and the perpetual smile on his face made him instantly likable. He was not a scholar; he was happy just being an average student and surrounded by a bevy of his dedicated friends.

Roger Sherwood was the polar opposite of Manny. He was thin with light brown hair, brown eyes and was about the same height that I was (five feet, nine inches tall). He had a penchant for the fine arts and music; he could paint, was a competent sculptor, and played the piano well. The only athletics that he was interested in was the spectator sports; he said that his body hurt just by watching contact sports. Roger was a good conversationalist; he had a deep bass voice and he used it well when communicating with anyone. He could hold us spellbound for long periods of time with his conversations and unique humor. Roger was an only child and received everything that he asked for in the furtherance his educational interests which gave him opportunities that few of us had.

Charley Black was probably one of the most respected persons in our close knit group. Like me, he was interested in the natural sciences; but unlike me, he hated the literary arts. He was soft-spoken and could easily charm the ladies who loved to be around him at parties and other events. He was the shortest of us at five feet seven inches tall. He was stocky with broad shoulders and had the looks of an outdoorsman. His red hair was always disheveled and his eyes were a "burning blue," as Roger would say. He loved the outdoors and pursued his passions of fishing and hunting. He said that he would rather be a bear than a human so that he could eat full time and sleep it off during winter.

The fun started as soon as the four of us got together in a conversation or as a group to kibitz with other friends.

"Hey Judy! I heard that your poodle skirt was mysteriously torn at the Auburn Drive-In last night. Want to talk about it?" asked Manny.

"Yes it was. Don't you wish that it was you that ripped it off?" asked Judy.

"Not me, I don't mess around with virgins."

"And how would you know whether or not I was a virgin?"

"By the way you walk. Guys can tell, you know."

"Stuff your snide remarks in your shorts, you pervert, because that is the only thing that you would find there."

"Manny, you are not going to win this one," said Roger. "Give it a rest while you are still ahead."

"Hey, Lola baby, have we got a date tonight," asked Charley.

"Don't you wish!" said Lola. "I would rather date Tarzan's monkey than go out with you. I would also have someone more intelligent to talk to."

"Tarzan doesn't have a monkey. It's a chimpanzee," said Charley.

"Even more intelligent to talk to," said Lola.

"Man, girls have changed. They are different than they were just a year ago," said Manny.

"Not different, Manny, more selective," I said with a laugh.

We were watching Judy, with her head hung low, walking toward her friends. She said something to them and they all turned and looked at us with a sneer. Judy walked to and fro a few times, stopped, and they stared at us again.

"Hey, Manny, you're right, Judy does walk like a virgin," said one of the girls.

They all laughed loudly and walked toward the classroom at the sound of the first bell.

As we took our seats, Miss Goodman walked in. She was dressed in a tight blue skirt that was up to her knees, a white blouse, and a matching blue jacket. Everyone, including the girls, was stunned at how she looked. She was not dressed in the accepted style of the day, and the girls were both pleased and shocked at the surprise. Of course she had all of the guy's attention.

"I can't wait for her to write something on the blackboard," Manny whispered. "I must see the other side of her."

As Miss Goodman began to speak, I could only understand a few words occasionally. I, and all of the other guys in the room, were so distracted that we were fearful that she would ask a question of one of us. Her lips seemed to move in slow motion and I watched all of her body movements as if I were reading a book. In what seemed like only minutes, she concluded her remarks.

"Are there any questions?" she asked.

Not one person spoke. We sat there frozen in time, and we were clueless as to what she had said.

"If there are no questions, then we will move on," she said.

"What was the significance of the four corners of the Egyptian pyramids?" she asked.

"They pointed in the direction of North, South, East, and West," I said.

"When they buried the Pharaoh, in what position was his body placed?" she asked.

"I know, I know," said Manny. "He was placed horizontally."

Everyone laughed.

"Wrong answer," she said. "We will discuss that tomorrow. I will give you the first opportunity to answer the question tomorrow, Manny, so be prepared."

The bell rang at noon, and we all went our own ways to have lunch. I headed for home which was only a stone's throw from school; my mom ran a little restaurant where she sold hot dogs, hamburgers, and snacks, and it was busy this time of day. I grabbed a hamburger and an RC, and had a quick lunch. Everyone was to gather in the school yard after lunch, and I had to hurry back to join my friends. It was our favorite time of day.

The weather was perfect, so the crowd was larger than usual. A number of girls were practicing the latest dance steps without the accompaniment of music. I was approached by many of them who asked me to dance. I joined them, but I felt uncomfortable; I could only slow-dance, and my movements were both awkward and out of sync. Dancing was just not my forte.

My friends were gathered in a huddle talking softly.

"What's going on fellas?" I asked.

"You haven't heard?" asked Roger.

"Apparently I haven't," I said. "What?"

"The Principal came over and asked Miss Goodman to go home and change clothes. The old codger doesn't appreciate the female form."

"Will she be back today?" I asked.

"I suppose so. He came over at the start of lunch hour and talked to her. She will have plenty of time to change and be back soon."

"Well, the way that she was dressed was a pleasant distraction and I would have loved to have seen her dress that way every day. My whole day is now spoiled."

"Ours, too," everyone said in unison.

"It doesn't matter what she wears," said Manny. "I have my imagination and I can still fantasize as to what she looks like without ANY clothes."

Miss Goodman returned just before the lunch hour ended. She looked so dejected; that beautiful smile of hers disappeared and lines at the corners of her mouth formed when she frowned. I wanted to comfort her, but I knew that she would probably reject any sympathy from a student; that would no doubt get her into deeper trouble.

For the rest of the day, Miss Goodman did not say much. She said that we could study for the remainder of the day while she did some administrative work, but we knew that her heart was not into teaching after such a traumatic experience. With her head lowered, she attempted to hide her eyes with one hand while discreetly wiping tears from them with the other.

When the last bell rang, the classroom emptied quickly. After everyone left, I approached Miss Goodman.

"I heard what occurred today, and I am so sorry for everything that happened to you," I said. "I know that you are having a difficult day, and I would understand if you did not feel like coming to the Corlee Theater tomorrow."

"Oh, I will be there. I want to see the projection booth and watch you work for a while. That is if you still want me to come."

"Oh, I do want you to come. It gets a little lonely up there, and I look forward to seeing you. Incidentally, I was told that I could have up to two guests per day at the theater without charge. Tomorrow, I will start work at 12:00 noon and the movie starts at 1:00. There are a few things that I have to do before the movie starts."

"I will be there at noon, then."

Saturday morning I arose earlier than usual. After a hearty breakfast, I began my bathing and grooming routine. I wanted to

73

look especially good today. I used a little extra Brylcream, a splash more of shave lotion that I would have normally used, and I stared in the mirror longer than usual to assure that not one hair was out of place. I brushed my teeth and gargled with a mint flavored mouth wash, stepped out the door, and walked with a swagger toward the Corlee.

I arrived at the Corlee five minutes early and stood by the entrance waiting for the arrival of Miss Goodman. I continued to wait until 12:15, and I was disappointed that she had not yet arrived. I had to rush to the projection booth to perform my routines prior to the start of the movie. There was much to do: rewind all of the film that was delivered earlier that morning, clean the reflector mirror at the back of each projector, thread both projectors with film, and other necessary duties. With a sigh of relief, I finished all of my preliminary work by 12:40. The movie would start in just twenty minutes.

There was a knock at the projection room door. We kept that door locked with a chain inside the booth for security reasons. I opened the door and Miss Goodman looked at me and said, "Sorry I'm late. I had company this morning and couldn't get away."

"Did you have any problem getting into the theater?" I asked.

"Not at all. I told the manager that I was a friend of yours and he directed me to you. Did I miss anything?"

"Just a few preliminaries. The real work starts in fifteen minutes. I am so happy that you came. I finally have some company for at least a short period of time. The movie is a good one today. I think that you will enjoy it."

"How do you watch a movie from the projection booth? There are only two small observation windows beside each projector."

"Just outside the booth, there are seats where I can sit and watch the movie."

"Then I will sit and watch the movie with you."

I quickly showed her the projection booth, the equipment, and how it all worked together. I could not wait until those projectors were started so that I could sit next her and watch the movie.

Chapter 8

"Abandon the search for Truth; settle for a good fantasy."
Sir Arthur Conan Doyle

Miss Goodman watched closely as I began my routine for starting the movie. I described every step to her as I went about my duties.

"It is much different than I thought it would be," she said.

"Most people think that you just walk in, flip a switch on the projector and just sit back and watch the movie," I said. "I have to switch projectors every 20 minutes or so, but the audience does not know how and when it is done. It is accomplished through four steps by the projectionist and is done electronically. When you watch a movie, you will notice a round dot appearing on the upper right hand corner of the screen. That is a signal for the projectionist to perform two of four steps, and a second dot will appear about seven seconds later to signal the final steps to switch from one projector to the other, and that is to put it simply. After the switch-over, the other projector now has to be prepared for switching in another 20 minutes, on average. This goes on non-stop from the time the theater opens until it closes. I could go on for another 30 minutes and tell you much more, but you would get bored."

"I haven't gotten bored yet. I will go out and take my seat while you prepare for the start of the movie."

I started projector #1 which began to show the previews of coming attractions. I then went out of the booth and sat next to Miss Goodman.

"I enjoyed watching you work with the projectors. I am amazed at all that goes into showing a movie."

"The repetitiveness of it gets boring sometimes, but I like my job very much."

After the main feature started, Miss Goodman relaxed and seemed to enjoy the movie. I did not know at the time if she realized that her hand was on mine. She gave it a slight squeeze and then looked at me and smiled.

"Do you mind?"

"Oh, not at all. I rather like it."

"During a movie, and I don't know why, but I think that holding hands makes it more enjoyable, don't you?"

"It...It sure does," I said nervously.

"It would be even better if you put your arm around me."

I put my arm around her and she laid her head on my shoulder. I looked at her beautiful face and she reached up, put her hand behind my head, drew it toward her and kissed me. My blood felt as if it was boiling and perspiration was pouring down my face.

"Oh, Bobby Darrell, I have never been kissed like that before," she said. "Say you love me, Bobby. Oh, Bobby! Oh! Bobby!"

"Bobby, wake up! Wake up! It's time for the movie to start," said the manager, "it's 1:05."

"Where is Miss Goodman?" I asked.

79

"Miss Goodman?   Who is Miss Goodman?" replied the manager.

"Never mind.   I must have been dreaming. Sorry that I fell asleep; I did not get much sleep last night."

"Well, she did say that she would come," I thought.   "Something important must have come up."

After my shift ended, Manny, Roger, and Charley were waiting outside of the theater.

"Where are we going to tonight, to the Chicken Coop (our term for girl's favorite places to hang out)?" asked Manny.

"Not just yet," said Roger. "I would prefer to wait until later when the chicks get bored with the guys who have to go home early to their mommies. Then we can crow until midnight."

"Crow?   You are a regular Shakespeare, aren't you Roger?" said Charley.

"Who is Shakespeare?" asked Manny.

Here we go again, I thought. This is going to be difficult.

"Shakespeare was a poet and a playwright," I said. "He is the one who wrote Romeo and Juliet."

"Man, I don't know anything about Romeo and Juliet and Shakespeare. The only place that I ever saw that cat Shakespeare's name was on a fishing reel. Does he own that company?"

Figure 9. Shakespeare.

"No, he doesn't. Shakespeare lived about four hundred years ago and as far as I know he didn't even go fishing."

"There you go again talking about some cat who lived hundreds of years ago," said Manny. "Can't we talk about somebody living today, like Natalie Wood?"

"I promise you that we will later, Manny," I said. "We always talk about Natalie Wood at some point every time that we get together."

"Let's fly to the Chicken Coop, guys, and bless the chicks with our presence," I said. "There may be a few strays that we could have some fun with."

Before we arrived at our destination, I spotted Diana with her friend, Marci. She smiled and I looked in every direction to assure that her mom or dad was not in sight.

"Hi, Diana, I hope that everything is o.k. with you. I have missed you, and I am sorry that everything worked out the way that it did," I said.

"It was not your fault, it was mine," she said. "My parents have allowed me a little more freedom lately, but I am still not allowed to date."

"I understand. Maybe we could go for a walk sometime soon. That would be a harmless activity."

"I cannot even do that right now," she said with tears in her eyes. "I am sure that things will change for the better in the near future, but for now I must go. We will cross paths again soon."

"I am sure of that. I do hope to see you again soon."

As I turned to walk away, I heard a voice say, "We are going home now, Diana, hurry along."

The voice was a familiar one, and I did not look around to acknowledge the person; I did not want Diana to get into more trouble than she already was with her parents.

"Hey, guys, instead of going to the Chicken Coop, I just remembered that there is a party at Patsy Collins' tonight. We were not invited, but they might let us studs crash it," said Charley. "I know that the girls would love for us to be there."

"If they would have loved for us to be there, then why wouldn't they have invited us in the first place?" I asked.

"They probably just forgot us," said Roger. "That has to be the reason."

"Let's go before they start playing Post Office," said Manny. "I want to get into some kissing with those chicks before their lipstick wears off."

"You want their lipstick on your lips, Manny?" asked Roger. "I wouldn't want lipstick on my lips and look like a girl."

"Who said anything about it on my lips, Roger?" said Manny. "Man, you don't have any imagination at all."

"If you would ask a girl to kiss you some place other than your lips, it could cause your face to hurt considerably," I said.

"How could that cause my face to hurt?" asked Manny.

"From the hard right that she is going to give you in the chops when you ask her for that kiss," I said.

When we arrived at Patsy Collins' house, we heard a Little Richard record blaring through the record player speaker. It was so loud that we had to knock hard on the door. The room quieted; Patsy opened the door and with a sigh said, "Oh, thank God. I thought that you might be a neighbor coming to complain about the music being too loud."

"We thought that we would drop by and see how the party was going," I said tentatively.

"We are having a great time. We had a few that didn't show up. Would you all like to join us?"

"Sure," I said.

When we entered the house, we were surprised that there were far more girls than guys. I began to imagine the possibilities of a memorable night. I sat down on one of the couches and observed the activity. The guests looked as though they were bored and waiting for something to happen.

"May I sit here?" said Marci, a girl that I already had experience with playing

Post Office, as she pointed to a space next to me.

"Sure, Marci," I said. "I have not seen you since the birthday party that Diana gave me."

"Who are you with?"

"I came with a few friends."

"Do you have a date with you?"

"No. Diana and I broke up, as you well know."

"I know. What exactly happened?"

"It was just a misunderstanding. It may work itself out later."

"Diana's loss will be someone else's gain."

"I don't see it that way. I like Diana a lot, and she is going through a difficult time right now."

She stood, and as she did, she took my hand and tugged at it as a signal for me to stand.

"Let's go to the back porch. It is getting a little too stuffy in here for me," she said.

The back porch of the house faced a large lot with a vegetable garden and a tool shed. Neat rows of corn, tomato plants, cabbage, a large lettuce bed, and potatoes were the most prominent vegetables in the garden. Toward the fence line at the rear of the garden, I spotted two raccoons; they were scurrying to and fro looking for an evening meal. The air was pleasantly cool, and I could smell the fragrances of the many flowers that were planted around the house. I could also smell Marci's perfume which had a similar odor to that of the brand that Miss Goodman used.

"That is a wonderful perfume that you are wearing. It is similar to Miss Goodman's."

"It is the same. I splashed some on when I heard your voice a few minutes ago. I knew that you would like it."

Chapter 9

Two wymen in one howse,
Two cattes and one mowce,
Two dogges and one bone,
Maye never accorde in one.
Old English proverb.

We stood on the back porch for about twenty minutes, and I could tell that Marci had something on her mind.

"Could I ask you a question?" said Marci. "I know that it is only a rumor, but did you...."

"No, I did not have sex with Diana," I said emphatically. "Everyone asks me that question. I do not want to talk about it, Marci! Even if I had, I would not tell anyone about it. Gossip will destroy Diana if this continues, and I do not want to hear any of it."

"Sorry! I didn't mean anything by it. I was just wondering if it was just a rumor or the truth."

"It is a rumor, and I do not want to say any more about it."

"I like you," she said. "Is there any chance that we could get together sometime for a walk or movie."

"Sure. Tomorrow is Sunday and I start to work at 12:00 noon. The movie starts at 1:00, and we can watch it together. Just tell them at the entrance that you are a friend of mind and they will direct you"

"I will be there."

As I turned to leave, she looked up at me and smiled.

"May I have a kiss before you leave?" she asked.

"Sure, I suppose that I could sacrifice myself to a gorgeous creature like yourself," I said jokingly.

She pulled me as close to her as she could, tilted her head back, and gave me a passionate kiss. She was reluctant to let me go, and it took some effort to pull free from her.

"I will see you tomorrow at noon. Please try to be there on time."

I arrived on Sunday at the Corlee at 11:50 and I was surprised to see Marci waiting.

"I see that you made it," I said. "Let's go on up to the projection booth, and I will get started."

As soon as we got to the projection booth, the manager called me on the intercom.

"There is a Miss Goodman here to see you. Do you want me to send her up?" he asked.

"Oh, no!" I thought. "What should I do now?"

"Tell her that I will be down in a couple of minutes, and please tell her to wait."

"Marci, I need to ask a favor of you. Miss Goodman is here to see me about something. If you would, please go to the lower level, and I will come for you as soon as I can."

"Is everything o.k.?" she asked.

"Everything is cool."

"I will be sitting in the rear row so that I can be found easily."

Quickly, I went downstairs to escort Miss Goodman to the projection booth.

"I wasn't expecting you today," I said.

"I am sorry that I didn't make it yesterday, but I had a little emergency. I didn't think that you would mind if I came today."

"Not at all. I am happy to have you here."

I opened the door to the projection booth, and she was surprised at how large it was. She began to inspect the projectors, the reel drawers, the rewind station, and the film repair equipment.

"I feel like that I am in a film studio. This is not at all what I expected," she said.

After explaining the equipment to her, I looked at my watch and said, "Showtime!"

I started the #1 projector and the previews of coming attractions began.

"Are you going to stay for the movie?" I asked.

"I plan to. May I sit outside of the projection booth and watch it?"

"Have a seat and I will be with you in about two minutes. I still have a couple of things to do."

When I went out to join her, she had already surmised that I would require the end seat, so she moved over to the next one.

"This is a great place to watch the movie; the screen looks really small from up here, but I like it, though," she said.

"Let me say again, I am so happy that you stopped by. I love to have company up here; it gets lonely with no one to talk to. Today, I will be here for six hours."

"I know what you mean. No one knows better than I do as to what that feels like. I am single, you know."

"Yes, I know. I had heard that you were single, but I did not believe it at first. You are such a beautiful woman and if I were your age, I would be knocking on your door every day."

She smiled and said, "What is the situation with you and Diana?"

"I can only say that we may never get back together. Her parents are keeping a close eye on her."

"Such a shame! I know that you like each other a lot."

Time flew by so quickly that the end of the movie caught me by surprise. There was a double feature so I asked her if she was going to stay for the second feature.

"No, I must be going. Maybe some other time. I loved the time that I spent with you."

As she got up to leave, she put her arms around me and hugged me tightly. I had this beautiful woman in a hug, and my mind went blank; I had no idea as to what I should do next. When she relaxed the hug and returned her arms to her side, I was disappointed. I wanted her to stay more than ever now.

"I will see you Monday morning," she said. "Maybe we can do this again soon."

As she was leaving, I thought about Marci. I had completely forgotten about her, and I was doubtful that she would still be in the theater. I rushed downstairs and I was pleased that she had not left.

"I'm sorry, Marci," I said. "I did not forget about you, but Miss Goodman stayed longer than I thought she would."

"What in the world were you two talking about? It sure must have been important."

"Yes. It was very important."

On Monday morning, I could not stop looking at Miss Goodman. Recalling yesterday at the Corlee, I kept thinking of the hug that she gave me and the warmth of her body next to mine. I must forget yesterday, I thought. She is my teacher and much older than I am, and to think that she would care for me any more than she would any of her other students would be ludicrous. From this moment on, I will be more formal with her and direct my attention elsewhere.

After lunch, everyone gathered in the schoolyard as usual. The girls followed their usual routine of practicing the newest dance steps, and the guys were looking on with interest. They were dancing without music, so Manny and Charley started singing the Gene Vincent song, "Be-bop-a-lula," and swinging their hips like Elvis.

"Give it up you two," I said. "Neither of you are ever going to be an Elvis."

"What does he have on me?" asked Manny. "I may not have his looks, voice, charisma, money, cars, girls, and mansion....well, maybe you're right. But I am charming in my own way."

"I heard that," said Roger. "You are as charming and personable as Frankenstein's monster."

"Who do you think is better looking: Boris Karloff, Lon Chaney, or me?" asked Charley.

"I would say that you look more like Lon Chaney AFTER he changes into the werewolf in the movie 'Wolf Man.' You have such cute canine teeth," said Manny.

"All the better to rip your heart out with," said Charley. "Be on the lookout for me at the next full moon."

Marci called my name. I turned and saw her walking toward me. This is just not my day, I thought. I did not feel like talking to her right now. I was looking for some escape.

"What's up, Marci?" I asked.

"I would like to see the movie at the Corlee tonight. Could you use some company while you are working?"

"I have a lot on my mind today, Marci. You may watch the movie, but if I appear distant tonight, it will not be because I am upset at you. My hours are 4:00 to 7:00, so be there on time."

Marci arrived at the theater a little early. She was in a happy mood; she smiled, took my hand, and we walked up to the projection booth. After I readied the two projectors for the evening's movie I had some time to sit with her and talk. She cracked a joke, which I did not hear, and she laughed loudly at the punch line. I laughed as though I heard the joke.

"Is there anything wrong? I get the feeling that you would prefer to be alone."

"No, I am happy that you are here. If I were alone, I would have too much time to think about the unpleasant things that are bothering me."

"I could cheer you up even more if you would only give me a chance."

"Sounds good to me. I need cheering up."

"Then let me know when you want to come over to my house. You won't be disappointed."

Chapter 10

"Shared joy is a double joy; shared sorrow is half a sorrow."
Swedish Proverb

It was finally the end of the school year. The year was 1957 – a pivotal point in all of our lives. We graduated from the eighth grade, and would be attending our first year of high school beginning the first part of August. I turned 15 years old, but I felt much older. I had a wonderful job, which carried a lot of responsibility, and I was saving money to buy my first car at this time next year.

After the last bell, everyone was ready for the summer break. We walked out of the classroom and gathered in the schoolyard to say our goodbyes for the summer. We would not see many of our schoolmates during the summer, so it was a bittersweet moment for us.

I went back into the classroom to say goodbye to Miss Goodman. As I approached her, she smiled and said, "I am going to miss this class. It has been the best class that I have ever taught. I am sure going to miss everyone."

"I will miss you, Miss Goodman. I think that you are not only a great teacher, you are also a great person. I wish you the very best."

"I will not be saying goodbye to you yet. I will continue to see you at the Corlee if you will allow me to. I love watching the movies from the balcony."

"Come anytime. My hours through the week will be the same as the week-end during the summer. And you know the password to get in free," I said with a chuckle.

"I will be there often, you can count on it. It gets lonely sitting in my house with nothing to do. The movies offer an escape for me."

"See you soon, then. You do not have to let me know in advance, just come on up anytime."

I went back to the schoolyard. Almost everyone had left except Marci.

"Had to say goodbye to your girlfriend, huh?" she asked.

"Don't I wish," I said jokingly.

"I am going to Saw Mill Hollow (not far past the Corlee). I will walk with you to the Corlee."

We were walking at a slow pace since I had plenty of time before my shift started. I felt relieved that school was out for the summer, but I had no plans for any recreational activities during the summer break.

"Would you like to come to my house after work?" It looks as though you might need some company to cheer you up."

"What do have in mind? If I come, I would not want to sit and do nothing."

"Don't worry about that. I have a new record player and lots of great records. We will listen to them and slow dance, because I know that is the only type of dance that you like to do. We could play cards, talk, or do anything else that you would want to do."

"I cannot promise you anything. Let me think about it. If I decide to come, I will be there no later than 7:15."

"I look forward to it," she said.

The day seemed to never end. This was one of those rare times when I wished that I was not working and had the freedom to do as I pleased. But if I were not working, there would be a danger that I would become overly bored. Maybe I should go and see Marci after my shift. At least I would have her company and participate in some activities, though small as they seemed.

I arrived at Marci's house at the time that I told her that I would be there. I could hear her record player blaring; she had the sound turned up so loud that she did not hear me knock on the door. I had to wait until the end of the record that she was playing before I knocked loudly again.

"I hear you, I hear you," she screamed loudly. "I'm coming."

"Oh, I am sorry that I didn't hear you," she said as she opened the door. "I actually did not expect you this evening. Come on in."

"Where is everybody?" I asked.

"My mom and dad are out for the evening. They will not be back until late tonight."

"Did they know that there was a possibility that I would be here?"

"No, and I didn't either. Don't worry, we will be all right."

She invited me into her bedroom where she kept her record player.

"I would prefer to go to the living room. If your parents came home early, I certainly would not want to be caught in your bedroom."

"Good point. Help me move my record player and records in there. We will have more room to dance. That is, if you want to."

"We will see," I said.

"What records do you like?" she asked.

"I like all types of music. You be the DJ for the evening."

She played the record "It's not for me to Say" by Johnny Mathis, a song that I loved.

"Now I could dance to this," I said.

I put my arms around her. She pulled me as close to her as she could and as we danced, she looked up at me.

"There is no one that I would rather be with than you right now. I want to kiss you so much," she said.

"You are gorgeous, Marci, I wouldn't object to that."

We stopped dancing and she tiptoed to reach my lips and gave me such a long passionate kiss that I became breathless. She lifted her skirt to her waist and placed my hands on her buttocks.

"Hold me close to your body. Right now, I feel that I want all of you." she said.

"Let's go to the couch.   It is more comfortable there."

As we moved toward the couch, she put her arms around me and kissed me with those wonderful full lips. When we sat down, her tongue began to explore every part of my lips and mouth. She placed my hand on her breasts and squeezed them. The excitement was almost too much for me; we were breathing heavily and I felt that the passion we had for each other at that moment was endless. She was so excited that she took my hand from her breast and placed it on her crotch.

"Oh, my!" she said. "I am ready to explode. Keep doing that! Yes. Oh....!"

She relaxed and laid back as though she was exhausted. She looked at me and smiled.

"Did you enjoy that?" she asked.

"Oh, I did! It was terrific, but I am concerned that your parents will walk through that door at any moment and catch us in the act."

"There is no possibility of getting caught. My parents are gone for the entire evening."

I was beginning to feel uneasy. What would her parents do or say to her if they found out about our lovemaking? This was far more serious than what Diana and I did.

"Marci, I think that I had better go. It is getting late and I do not want your parents to discover me here."

"We still have plenty of time. I don't want you to leave. I am having too much fun."

"I am having fun also, but I must go. I promise that I will be back soon. I enjoyed myself, but I don't want to risk the possibility of your parents suddenly walking through that door."

As I walked to the door, I saw the headlights of a car approaching. I had plenty of time to leave and escape a surprise like the one that I received at Diana's. I began to walk at a normal pace down the street. I looked up briefly; it was her parents returning from their visit.

It was not too late to walk to the Big Top and meet with friends or anyone else there that I might know. There were a few people gathered in small groups, but none that I knew. I ordered a slice of apple cobbler and a cup of coffee which I consumed expeditiously.

I looked around the restaurant and observed the many differences in such a small number of people. A large family, along with friends, sat at one table where there was banter, smiles, and the enjoyment of each other's company. They were recalling memories of recent events and the happy times that each of them had had over the years. The pleasantry was uplifting and the friendships were obviously close and long-lasting.

At another table, a family of four with two pre-teen girls had the look of gloom on their faces. Their conversations were focused on all of the negatives that each had experienced not only recently, but far back into their past. It depressed me so much that I turned my head away from them and tried to ignore any conversation that could be heard among them.

At another table, there was family of five that did not speak to, or look at, anyone or each other. They consumed their meals hurriedly with their heads lowered and left the restaurant without acknowledging anyone.

Maybe someday I would understand the vast differences in the personalities of people, I thought. But for now, those differences were just a few of the many mysteries of life that was left for me to explore.

Chapter 11

"Always obey your parents - when they are present."
Mark Twain

Shortly after school ended for the summer, the manager of the Auburn Drive-In asked me become his projectionist for the summer on Friday, Saturday, and Sunday evenings. I did not want to work evenings at the Auburn because the hours were too long for me. The movie could not be shown until dark, which was 8:30 P.M. or later, so after a double feature and repeating the main feature, as was the routine, it could be 1:00 A.M. or later when the drive-in closed. I protested, but I was offered a sizable increase in pay if I would take the job. Reluctantly, I did. In addition, the Corlee manager wanted me to work from 12:00 noon to 5:00 P.M. on Saturdays and Sundays, and 6:00 P.M. until closing Monday through Thursday. Two jobs on the week-end may have been too much for me, but I decided that I would try it.

In celebration of my new-found job, I thought that I would treat Manny, Roger, and Charley to a meal at the Pine View on the

Saturday evening before I started to work at the Auburn. When we arrived, we knew exactly who would be there - the same ones always showed up. The Pine View and the Big Top were THE places to be for a gathering of a large number of teens. As soon as we walked into the Pine View, Manny immediately spotted Judy.

"Hey, Judy," he said, "are you still a virgin."

"If you were the only man on earth, I would always be a virgin," said Judy.

"Aw, don't be so hard on me Judy. Someday you will be begging for me when my ship comes in."

"When your ship comes in, I hope that I am at the bus station, you pervert."

"I keep telling you, Manny, you don't stand a chance with Judy," I said. "She has too much class for a guy like you."

"Judy loves the bad boys," said Manny. "I can be as bad as you want me to be, Judy, or a sweet lovable slave to your charms."

"I will accept you as a slave but not the type of slave that your dirty mind is thinking of."

"She's on to me as always. I will not bother you again this evening, my sweet Belle of Saw Mill Hollow, but I cannot make any promises tomorrow night."

"Thanks for the favor. Just make that NOT bothering me permanently and we will get along just fine."

"Oh, she is vicious, but I love her anyway."

"I guess this is your last Saturday night before the week-end work," said Roger. "Won't you miss your freedom?"

"I will. I won't have much time to spend with the opposite sex."

"True, but you are earning good wages for a fifteen year old. I found a job, but it doesn't pay as much as yours."

We all ordered burgers, shakes, and fries. I was so hungry that it did not take long for me to finish my meal. Roger, Manny, and

Charley apparently were as hungry as I was; they also gulped down their meals.

Just as we finished our meals, Miss Goodman walked in with a well-dressed, handsome man. He had movie star looks and his clothes looked expensive. He was tall, with black hair, and he walked with a sophisticated air about him. He was, no doubt, from out of town; I had never seen anyone in Cumberland dress as well as he did. He and Miss Goodman were laughing and enjoying each other's company.

"Looks like Miss Goodman got hooked up with a well-to-do dandy," said Roger. "His suit probably cost more than I earn in six months."

"I would say more like two years of your earnings," quipped Manny. "I would bet that he is a doctor, lawyer, or some other professional man."

"Looks like she certainly is happy. She deserves all the happiness that she can get," I said.

When we were ready to leave the restaurant, I walked over to say hello to Miss Goodman. As I approached her, she smiled and asked me to sit down.

"I must go. I am here with friends."

"I will be seeing you around. This is, by the way, my brother, Vince, who is visiting me for a couple of days."

"Oh, wonderful!" I thought. "Her brother. She is still unattached."

For a brief moment, I was actually jealous of Vince by thinking that he was romantically involved with Miss Goodman.

"What is wrong with me?" I thought. "I should not be thinking this way. A relationship with Miss Goodman would be impossible with a person my age. I must focus on other things like my job, friends, and high school to keep my mind distracted from this beautiful goddess. Restraint! I must exercise restraint!"

After exchanging pleasantries with Miss Goodman and Vince, I left the restaurant with my friends. This was to be my final evening out for the summer. I would be working at the Auburn three nights a week and at the Corlee for four nights and I intended to make this evening a memorable one. I started walking toward Marci's house.

The evening was cooling rapidly as I picked up my pace toward Marci's. The sight of the street lights of Cumberland were disappearing as I walked toward her house, which was in a small, steep hollow. It was so dark that I could not see the road and I slowed my pace considerably. I heard dogs barking in the distance which got louder as I approached the house where they were. I looked up and saw a woman peeking out the window attempting to see what the commotion was all about, but it was too dark for her to see me. As I walked past the house, the barking of the dogs ceased momentarily and then became silent when they no longer felt threatened by a passing stranger. By the fading sound of the dogs, I knew that I was close to Marci's house. A light on the front porch came on and I was relieved that I could see the road well enough to pick up my pace again. Marci met me at the front door.

"I knew that someone was coming here by the sound of the neighbor's dogs, but I didn't expect you," she said. "By listening to them as someone approaches, I can usually tell about how far away they are from my house. I am glad that you came. Come in and meet my parents."

"Oh, no," I thought. "I did not come to meet her parents. Now what do I do?"

She smiled as she took my hand and guided me through the door. I pretended that I had never seen the inside of the house before. After introducing her parents, she invited me to sit down on the sofa next to her.

"Marci tells me that you are a projectionist at the Corlee and Auburn Drive-In," said her dad. "That sounds like an important job."

"I think so. There are no movies without the projectionist. I really love the job. Starting tomorrow, I will be working

114

Friday, Saturday, and Sunday nights at the Auburn for the entire summer. I will also be working at the Corlee Monday through Thursday nights from 6:00 P.M. until closing which is generally 10:30 or 11:00, depending on the length of the movie, and 12.00 noon until 6:00 P.M. on Saturdays and Sundays."

"Sounds confusing to me," said her mother. "I would have trouble remembering a schedule like that."

Her dad looked at me suspiciously and I could sense that he was going to ask me an uncomfortable question.

"How long have you known Marci?" he asked.

"Since the first grade. We have been close friends since then."

"I was curious as to why you would want to see her at this hour. Was this a planned visit?"

"No, it was not planned. I thought that I would just drop by and talk to her for a few moments. I start my evening job soon, and I will not be seeing any of my friends frequently. I hope that it is all right with you."

"That is fine with me. You may stay until her curfew which will begin in two hours."

"We will be on the front porch," said Marci.

"I feel like a fool, Marci, lying to your dad like that. True, the visit was not planned; I came here for a date, but I couldn't say that. This is a perfect evening and I did not want to waste it by being alone."

"My dad is no fool. Believe me, he knows that you are here for a date."

"Let's sit on the swing awhile," she said. "Let's enjoy what time that we have left of the evening."

I put my arm around her; she looked into my eyes and smiled.

"Do you mind if I come to the Corlee tomorrow afternoon? I get so lonely in the summertime sitting at home with nothing to do. In between reels, we could do some things that both of us might enjoy."

"That would be fine! Remember that my starting time tomorrow at the Corlee is 12:00 noon. And what are those things that I might enjoy?"

"Would you prefer to know now or be surprised tomorrow?"

"I love surprises, especially coming from you."

"I will be there tomorrow at noon, then. Prepare for the best."

"Now that was an offer that I could not refuse," I thought.

Chapter 12

"Long hair will make thee look dreadfully to thine enemies, and
manly to thy friends."
Thomas Dekker

Sunday morning, I arose late in an attempt to get as much rest as I possibly could. A long day was ahead, and I dreaded the hours. I would start at the Corlee at noon and I would end my day at about 1:00 A.M. at the Auburn for a total of 13 hours. At least I had Marci's visit to look forward to.

The City of Cumberland was so peaceful and quiet on Sundays. Most businesses were closed except for essential services, such as, gas stations, some grocery stores, and restaurants. Because of Blue Laws, alcohol could not be sold, so all of the bars were closed, but you could buy it in Cumberland if you knew the location of the city's bootleggers and were willing to pay exorbitant prices for it; there were many of those well-known establishments scattered all around the city. Automobile traffic was almost nonexistent except for those who were driving on their way to or from church, or out for a Sunday drive. So peaceful. So quiet. I felt like walking from one end of town to the other, but I did not have the time.

When I arrived at the Corlee, Marci was waiting at the entrance for me.

"You are always predictable," she said. "When you say that you are going to be somewhere at a certain time, you are always there."

"Family trait," I said.

We went into the projection booth and I prepared the projectors for the day's activity. I had become so familiar with the routine that it took me much less time than usual. I had a half hour before the movie was to start.

Marci had already taken her seat outside of the booth. I sat next to her and she took my hand. I put my arm around her and kissed her lightly.

"What's up with you?" she asked. "You are not the same eager lover boy that you usually are."

"If I am not as eager, it is not because of you. I just feel so happy and at peace. I think of all the good things that are yet to come; I am saving money to buy a car at this time next summer, and I will start my first year of high school in August. I have a lot to look forward to."

"You won't forget me when you buy your car, will you?"

"Not at all. I will haul that cute little butt of yours all over Harlan County and beyond."

"O.k., now kiss me like you mean it. And don't hold back, if you know what I mean."

"I think that I know what you mean, but that may be a little difficult here."

"Leave it to me lover boy, I will take care of everything."

She gave me such a long, exciting, and passionate kiss that it took my breath away. I pulled myself away from her and she smiled.

"Sorry. I know that I overdo it sometimes, but I love to kiss."

"You are a passionate person, but we cannot be overly passionate here; there are too many people sitting in the balcony."

"Our loss. I guess that kissing will have to do for now."

"I wanted to come here for another reason today," she said. "Diana's parents are giving her more freedoms, and all that she talks about is you. Are you still interested in her?"

"No, not at this time. I do not think that her parents would want me, of all people, to be seeing her."

I could hear a sigh of relief from Marci and she did not try to hide it.

"Will you see me often, then? I will always be there for you when you need me."

I thanked her for her devotion, but I did not want to have a steady girlfriend at this time; there were too many good things happening in my life and I did not feel

121

comfortable in having restrictions of any kind that would obligate me in any way.

"Yes, I will see you as often as I can, but I don't know how often. I am a busy person."

She turned her head away from me and wiped her eyes. I did not know if they were tears of joy or sadness. I did not dare ask.

The summer was slipping away fast, and school would be starting soon. I took some time to look around the various stores in Cumberland in search of clothes, shoes, and accessories for high school. I wanted something special, not the traditional styles that the other freshmen would be wearing. I wanted to stand out above everyone else, and I had the means to do it.

I bought a dark red jacket with black stripes for cool days, tight fitting jeans that were too long (we greasers loved to roll up our pants, which was one of our trademarks), a pair of black Italian style shoes with a buckle, various colored shirts with large collars, a wide leather belt, a leather jacket for the cold months, and a pair of sunglasses that were similar to the ones that Marlon Brando wore in "The Wild One." I also stocked up on combs (I kept losing them), Brylcream, and a top brand of shave lotion. I was now ready to impress the freshmen class and teachers of Cumberland High School.

Then, I went to the barber shop.

I wanted my hair to be long and combed back in a duck tail. Not knowing much about how barbers styled hair it was difficult to communicate with him. I sat in the chair and I was not fully prepared for his questions.

"How would you like your hair to be cut today?" he asked.

"I would like it long," I said.

"How long?"

"I don't really know. I want it long enough to be combed into a duck tail."

"I understand. You want the sides long. How about the top? How long do you want it?"

Figure 10. "I want an Elvis haircut."

I was getting frustrated. I knew what I wanted, but there was a communication problem with the barber. I was ready to give up when I had an epiphany.

"I want an Elvis haircut!"

"Now I know what you mean. Anytime that you come in from now on, always ask for an Elvis style haircut and I will know exactly what to do."

"One last thing. Do you want your sideburns long or short?"

"Just like Elvis!"

After leaving the barbershop, I met Manny, Charley, and Roger at the Pine View. This would be our last outing before school started, and they were as excited as I was. Each of them had also visited the barber, but their hair was much shorter than mine. Roger had a crew cut, which was also popular in the 50s.

"Man, I am ready for school," said Manny. "I am so tired of having nothing to do."

"You understand that you actually have to work in high school," said Charley. "It won't be like junior high. I heard that we will have a lot of homework that will keep us busy, Manny."

"That means that I will have to cut back on my social life," said Manny.

"What social life?" I asked. "I thought that you broke up with Sara. Or did she break up with you?"

"She broke up with me, man. I tried to lift her skirt, and she hit me on the head

125

with her Ricky Nelson doll," said Manny. "I could never understand girls."

"That is all you did?" I asked. "That doesn't sound like grounds for a break-up to me."

"Well, I also put my hand up her blouse and tried to cop a feel of those big, beautiful breasts of hers," said Manny.

"That still does not sound like Sara," said Charley. "I heard that she loves to have those visions of loveliness fondled."

"Well, actually it was everything at once," said Manny. "I lifted her skirt, put my hand up her blouse, and then climbed on top of her. Her dad caught us in the act, told me to get out of his house, and never return again. That is when she broke up with me. Her dad forced her to."

"You are lucky her dad didn't shoot you," I said. "I heard that he is not a tolerant man."

"Oh, well," said Manny. "Now I have to get another girlfriend. Know anyone?"

"If we did, we would not recommend anyone to you," said Charley with a loud laugh. "It is like Judy keeps saying, man, you are a real pervert."

We talked for about an hour. I hated to leave, but my shift at the Corlee was about to begin. Monday was the big day; the beginning of my first year at Cumberland High School.

Chapter 13

"I have never let my schooling interfere with my education."
Mark Twain

Monday morning, I awoke early to get ready for school. I wanted to look my best and make a good impression on my teachers and classmates.

After bathing, I dressed in a new pair of jeans, a matching shirt, and my new shoes. I squeezed more than a little dab of Brylcream on my hand, smeared it on the other hand and applied it to my hair with my fingers. I took my comb and stood in front of the mirror for a long time continuously combing it to assure that every hair was in place. I did the same with my sideburns. I took one final look in the mirror and approved of my new image. I walked out of the house toward Cumberland High School, and I felt as though I was walking on air.

I arrived about twenty minutes early so that I could do some exploring of my new digs before first bell. I had registered the previous week, so I knew what room number to report to; it was obvious who the freshmen were by the helter-skelter way that they searched for their homeroom.

The school still had that familiar smell of a new building although it had been built eight years prior. The hallways, walls, lockers, and everything in sight looked new, and the lighting was a major improvement over the elementary and junior high

Figure 11. Cumberland High School.

buildings. I went to my assigned locker, placed my school supplies in it, and locked it with my newly purchased lock.

Manny, Charley, and Roger were in a huddle talking low but laughing loudly.

"What's up?" guys, I asked.

"Man, you should see this place," said Charley. "Talk about a Chicken Coop!

129

The entire school has more gorgeous chicks than Hollywood Boulevard."

"You have never been to Hollywood Boulevard, but you may be right about the chicks," said Roger.

"I like the older ones," said Manny. "I said hello to a girl who is a junior or senior, and she actually said hello back to me."

"She doesn't know you yet, Manny," I said. "If she speaks to you again in a week, you could have a remote chance with her if she said two words to you instead of one."

"I've got to get a date soon, man," said Manny. "Surely, there is some girl in this school that is longing for me."

"There's the bell, guys. Good luck," I said.

I walked into my homeroom and looked around as everyone was being seated. There was not much of a choice in seating; I arrived a little too late to choose whom I would sit next to.

"Hi," I said to Judy, the girl that Manny often harassed verbally.

"Hi. I am glad that you are sitting next to me," she said. "I am so nervous about high school."

"Don't worry, everything will be just fine. Just think that you are back on the hill in the old wooden buildings."

"Heaven forbid, I hated those old fire traps. I feel much better in this building; it is the academic part that I worry about. I have heard some horror stories about how hard high school is and all the homework that we will be doing."

"I don't know who told you that. There are some people who say it is hard, but someone as smart as you will have no problem. I will give you any help that I can if I have the time. That is if you really need it."

"I appreciate that. If you don't mind, I will call on you from time to time."

"Silence, please!" said our homeroom teacher. "When you hear the bell, I expect total silence. There will be no gum chewing, spitting, whispering, passing notes, cheating on tests, the flicking of hair on the person in front of you, or any other errant behavior. We don't use a paddle in high school, but I have a principal down the hall that I can send you to, and he could make your life miserable if he really wanted to."

I knew the principal's reputation as a disciplinarian. He was also my cousin via of my Grandma Mary Huff-White, and I would never want to go to his office for anything. Outside of school, though, he was a different person.

There was much to like about the first few weeks of high school. I was surprised, though, at the number of students who had a difficult time adjusting to the high school curriculum. I had to work harder, but I adjusted well to the heavier load of homework, but some of my classmates did not expect the extra amount of effort required in high school. Some were just lazy and some did not like school at all and would later drop out as soon as they reached the age of sixteen. For most of us, high school was an adventure that we looked forward to.

As the weeks passed, Judy Cassidy invited me to her house for a party with a limited number of her friends. I had to decline because of my evening working hours, but I invited her to come to the Corlee on a Saturday or Sunday when my shift started at noon.

"I will do that someday," she said.

Judy was a pretty girl, who had a lot of friends, but did not date much. She was about the same height that I was with shoulder length wavy hair, which was always

Figure 12. Lauren Bacall.

styled similar to that of Lauren Bacall's. She was one of a few in her circle of friends who set aside time in the evening for the intense study of her homework assignments. She was ambitious and although she started high school fearful of the coming barrage of homework, she adapted well and quickly.

Judy was an ideal "Peggy Sue," a generic name that we gave to girls when we talked about them in general and no one in particular. A Peggy Sue was an idealized version of a girl with the looks of Natalie Wood, the devotion and housekeeping skills of June Cleaver (of the "Leave it to Beaver" television show), and the loyalty of Lassie.

I could not wait for a visit from her at the Corlee.

As late fall approached, the Auburn closed until the following spring. I felt a great deal of relief that I did not have to work those long week-end hours. While I loved my job, it was interfering with my school work and social life.

Especially my social life.

The following Saturday, Manny, Charley, Roger and I decided to throw a party of our own, but we had no place for the type of party that we wanted to have.

"I know the perfect place," I said. "We could have it at our old swimming hole on Cloverlick. We could make as much noise as we wanted and have a lot of fun."

"Would the girls trust us with a party at a place like that?" Roger asked. "I could think of some possibilities that would make Clark Gable blush."

"Let's spread the word about the party to everyone that we know, Roger. We may be surprised as to who might show up," I said.

"We must invite Richard and Linda," said Manny. "We could listen to music on his car radio."

"Brilliant, Manny," said Charley. "You are so bright that you may someday win the Nobel Prize."

"What is a noble prize?" asked Manny. "I have never heard of it."

"It is a NOBEL prize, Manny, not a NOBLE prize," I said. "The prize is given for certain outstanding contributions to mankind and it is worth more than you could ever earn in a lifetime."

"Is it some type of quiz show?" asked Manny. "Because if it is, I would never get the prize. I don't even have the answers for most of my tests in school."

"Never mind, Manny," Roger said. "We can talk about that later."

The word spread quickly that there was going to be a party at the swimming hole. When we arrived, there were at least thirty-five people milling about. Those who came without a date were attempting to pair up with someone for the evening. Judy was the first to approach me.

"Do you have a date?" she asked.

"No, I do not. Would you want to risk being seen with me?"

"Most certainly!"

"Let's go and say hello to everyone," I said. "It is getting so dark and I am having a difficult time seeing people's faces. I think that it is time to build a bonfire."

We gathered wood from around the creek bank, piled it high and set it aflame. It took the chill off the cool, moonless night and attracted the partygoers closer to the fire's warm, bright flames. As everyone gathered around the fire, they danced to the sounds from the car radio. The creek could be heard faintly flowing over rocks, large and small, creating that familiar sound of rushing water, putting me into an almost hypnotic trance. I put my arm around Judy and we swayed to a Johnny Mathis ballad. She looked up at me and brushed her lips tentatively against mine. The flicker of the fire showed her beautiful face in an eerily different light that made her look even more beautiful. I kissed her lips lightly; she looked up, smiled, and held me in a long tight hug.

"Let's get away from the fire for a few minutes," she said. "I would prefer to be alone with you right now."

As we walked a short distance from the fire, we saw a couple in the darkness kissing passionately. The world did not exist to them at the moment; nothing else seemed to matter, not even us, who were observing them. When they saw us, they began to walk toward the fire. I looked at the girl, and I was surprised to see her there.

"Hi, Marci," I said.

Chapter 14

"There may be a great fire in our soul, yet no one ever comes to
warm himself at it, and the passers-by see only a wisp of smoke."
Vincent van Gogh

Hi, Bobby Darrell," she said nervously. "I didn't expect you here tonight."

"Likewise.   Are   you   enjoying yourself?"

"Well….I…..guess so. Are you?" she asked tentatively.

"Yes, I am," I said, as I turned to walk toward the bonfire.

She began to tremble as she and her date followed us to the bonfire. She tried to speak to me, but her words were spoken so softly that I could not hear her.

"I cannot understand what you are saying, Marci. Maybe we could get together some other time and chat."

"Could I talk to you alone for a couple of minutes? I have something to say to you."

"I'm sorry, Marci. I am here with Judy and it would be rude for me to leave her and talk to you in private. We will talk soon."

She turned to her date, said something to him, and they left the party.

The party continued well into the night. We sat around the bonfire enjoying

Figure 13. What is a party without a bonfire?

quiet moments with our dates before the end of a wonderful evening. Judy laid her head on my shoulder and sighed as the fire dwindled to a glowing ash and then, in what seemed like a brief time, a gray, cool mass.

Most of the partygoers were saying their goodbyes as the night became cooler and curfews were becoming dangerously close for some of the girls. I kissed Judy goodbye and she left with her friends.

Then, I thought of Marci. "What exactly did she want to talk to me about? I am sure that I will find out soon," I thought.

Monday morning came too quickly for me. It was time for the mid-term exams and I felt as though I was not ready for them. This was the first mid-terms for us freshmen, and no one knew what to expect. We were all skittish and there were not many smiles among us.

As the tests were distributed, I heard groans long before anyone looked at them. The anticipation of difficult questions that no one could answer ran rampant even among the most intelligent of the students. At the direction of our teacher, Mr. Connors, we opened the cover page of the test. Not too bad, I thought, it is much easier than I could have imagined. I finished the test long before the allotted time, handed it to the teacher, and left the classroom. Feeling a great sense of relief, I walked outside of the building into the cool, fresh air. As the door slammed behind me, I heard a familiar voice.

"How did you do on the test?" asked Marci.

"Very well. It wasn't easy, but it was easier than I thought. I was curious as to what you wanted to talk to me about. I'm all ears."

"I just wanted to talk about Saturday night at the party. I am sorry that you saw me with Billy. He asked me to go the party with him and I agreed, but I didn't think that it would go as far as it did. Are you angry with me?"

"Not at all! Why should I be? We are not committed to any relationship that would prevent either of us from dating anyone that we wanted. Remember, I also had a date with Judy Cassidy."

"Does that mean that you aren't interested in me? I was hoping that we could get together often."

"I am interested in you as a close friend, Marci. I never made any promises that would go beyond that."

"May I continue to see you at the Corlee? I love to go there and watch movies with you."

"You may if I do not have another guest there, but you must let me know well in advance."

"O.k.," she said. "I will."

She turned and walked away indignantly. I did not mean to hurt her, but I thought that she was acting immaturely.

As the day advanced, I took a total of five mid-term exams and I was getting weary. When the last test was completed, I felt a great sense of relief. If the mid-terms drained that much energy from me, the finals should exhaust me even further, I thought.

Classes ended after the mid-terms for a welcomed break. Many of us gathered at the Big Top for a celebration. The restaurant was packed with students and teachers alike. Everyone had a smile on their faces, and we all felt relaxed and refreshed.

"I thought that those tests would never end," said Manny. "Those questions were tricky to me."

"What do you mean tricky?" I asked. "I wasn't fooled by any of the questions."

"Well, one of the questions was about Julius Caesar. It asked what he was best known for, and the only thing that I could come up with was Caesar Salad. Where else could it come from except Julius Caesar?"

"I don't think that the term Caesar Salad came from Julius Caesar," said Roger. "We will just have to wait until we get our test grades back for the correct answer. I said that he was best known as a military genius and General, and not so much as an Emperor."

"Uh, oh! Look who's here," said Charley. "She's coming through the door now."

It was Miss Goodman. She walked toward the other teachers who were sitting in an area reserved especially for them. I looked over at her and marveled at her beauty. She glanced around the room and waved to everyone before she sat down.

"That is one of the most beautiful women that I have ever seen," said Manny. "She looks just like Audrey Hepburn."

"Every woman is always the most beautiful one that you have ever seen, Manny," I said, "but I will have to agree with you about Miss Goodman. She has the looks and figure that would win any beauty contest."

"There goes my imagination again," said Manny. "I am undressing her now. She just took off her blouse and is now unsnapping her bra. Nice breasts! She is now taking off her half-slip. What an amazing body. She is now reaching for her panties. Oh, yes! Tonight, when I go to bed, I will continue where I just left off."

"Manny, you have a wild and rich imagination," said Roger. "Could I borrow some of it tonight when I go to bed?"

"Dream on guys," I said. "Miss Goodman would not give either of you the time of day. I'll bet that she is as chaste as Sandra Dee."

"Sandra Dee? She is one of the most beautiful women that I have ever seen," said Manny.

"Knock it off, guys. She's coming our way," said Roger.

"Hello, Roger, Charley, Manny, Bobby," she said. "Enjoying your break from school?"

"Yes," we all said in unison. "Very much so."

"You all have a wonderful evening," she said, as she walked out the door.

"If I could go home with her, my every fantasy would come true," said Manny.

"What is wrong with Marci lately," said Charley. "She seems depressed about something. She keeps mumbling something about the party that we had at the swimming hole."

"I don't know Charley," I said. "She may be having trouble with the guy that she was with at the party."

I said that knowing that the problem she was having was with me. Maybe I should talk to her soon. She may need someone to comfort her.

The next day was Saturday. I spent most of the morning relaxing before my shift began at the Corlee. I did not want to work that day, but I felt obligated to. If I missed my shift on any day, the person that worked nights would have to work a double shift. He had missed some days himself and I was called on the work a double shift, which was tiring and boring.

As usual, the town was busy on Saturdays. The grocery stores, Meyer's Hardware, the Western Auto Store, Fugate's Drug store, and every other store in town was packed. All of the parking spaces from one end of town to the other were occupied. The liquor stores were exceptionally busy on Saturdays supplying bootleggers from the surrounding counties, where the sale of alcoholic beverages was illegal, with their inventory for the following week which they marked up by 100% or more. There were lines at most of the gas stations; Cumberland was the only place in a wide area, including Benham and Lynch, where gasoline could be purchased. And one of the busiest places in town was the Corlee Theater. On Saturdays, in addition to a double feature, three or four more cartoons than usual and a serial would be shown at a bargain price. I was ready to supply the entertainment.

As I walked through the entry door of the theater, the manager said that there was a Leslie Goodman there to see me, and he directed her to the projection booth.

What a wonderful afternoon this is going to be, I thought.

Chapter 15

"A gift consists not in what is done or given, but in the intention of
the giver or doer."
Seneca

ood afternoon, Bobby," she said. "I wondered if you would like some company today. It got a little lonely around the house, so I thought that I would come and watch the double feature today."

"I am always happy to have company. The movies are going to be good ones today."

She came into the projection booth to watch me thread the machines and prepare for the days entertainment. She was watching closely as I hurried to complete my duties so that I could sit and talk to her. I had about thirty minutes remaining until show time; I had no idea as to what we could talk about.

"I have a gift for you," she said. "I picked it up on the way here. It is my way of thanking you for the free movies."

"That is not necessary. It doesn't cost me anything. I should buy you a gift for keeping me company."

She reached in her purse and pulled out a keychain with the name Bobby on it.

"In a few months, you will be buying your car. I thought that this would be an appropriate gift for you. Just don't tell anyone that I bought it for you."

"Don't worry about that. I understand."

"Are you going to take me for a ride when you get it?"

I knew that she was joking and teasing me at the same time.

"I look forward to it," I said with a wide smile.

At 1:00, I started projector #1 and quickly returned to my seat next to Miss Goodman. She was watching the movie and I was watching her. She was enjoying the movie as much as I was enjoying her reactions to it.

"I have been wanting to see 'The Bridge on the River Kwai' ever since it was released. I just love William Holden and Alec Guinness, don't you?"

"Yes, they are wonderful actors. The movie is a big success for us at the Corlee. We have been getting sizable audiences because of it."

After the change-over to the #2 projector and the preparation of #1 for the next change-over, I hurried back to my seat. After about ten minutes into the reel, I felt her head on my shoulder. I was thrilled beyond belief and I did not dare to move; I was fearful that she would take any movement by me as a signal to lift her head from my shoulder. So many things were going through my mind.

"What should I do?" I thought. "I want to sit like this forever."

"Should I put my arm around her?"

"No, that would be inappropriate."

"Should I say something - anything to her?"

151

"No, I think that I will just sit here and enjoy as much of her as I can."

She raised her head rapidly.

"Oh, sorry! I was so relaxed that I briefly fell asleep. Did I bother you by laying my head on your shoulder?"

"No, not all. I rather enjoyed it."

"Oh, no!" I thought. "Now I have said something that I shouldn't have said."

She looked up at me and smiled.

"You enjoyed it, huh?"

"I am sorry, I didn't mean to say that. I hope that I did not anger you or make you feel uncomfortable."

"No, not at all! Then you wouldn't mind if I did it again, would you?"

"Is she kidding or is she serious?" I thought.

"No! I wouldn't mind at all. As a matter of fact, my shoulder is yours for the rest of the day."

I was joking with her and I was surprised when she laid her head on my shoulder again and went to sleep. This is becoming one of the best days of my life, I thought, as I imagined that I was sleeping with her. In a way, I was.

Midway through the second movie, Miss Goodman was ready to leave the theater.

"I'm sorry. I am so tired that I must go home and rest. Thank you for the movie and the company. If you get lonely and want to come over to my house sometime, we could play cards, watch TV, or anything else that you might want to do."

Anything else that I might want to do? That sounds like an invitation that I couldn't refuse.

As my shift ended at 6:00, I went to Judy's house before I joined my friends at the Big Top. As I approached her house, I could hear a Chuck Berry record playing. There were many voices and giggling that could be faintly heard in the living room. I knocked on the door and she had to yell above the noise.

"Be right there!" she said.

She opened the door and stood frozen for a moment. She had her hair in curlers and was in her pajamas.

"We decided to have a pajama party tonight. Marci, Diana, Linda, and few other girls are here. Want to come in?"

"No. I will see you again soon."

I heard a familiar voice from one of the bedrooms.

"Don't let him leave, I want to talk to him," said Marci.

Marci was also in her pajamas and her hair in curlers.

"What's with the curlers?" I asked.

"We are styling each other's hair. We always do that at our pajama parties. What are you doing this evening?"

"I am going to the Big Top and join the guys."

"I can leave the party and we could go to my house if you want to. It is so boring here."

"I can't do that Marci. I have already decided to go to the Big Top. The guys will be waiting for me."

"That's fine. May I kiss you before you go?"

"Here? On the front porch?"

"We can go to the back porch. It is enclosed and private."

"O.k., but I have to leave soon.

The enclosed porch had two windows. She closed the blinds on both of them and held me in a tight hug. She kissed me as she always had – passionately. She loved to work her tongue while kissing, and I thought of the party at the swimming hole; did she kiss Billy in the same way that she is kissing me now? I would be naïve to think that she did not.

"I have to go. I hate to leave so soon but I have friends waiting for me. I will see you later."

"Maybe someday soon we will have our own pajama party."

"Sounds like fun. We will see."

On the way to the Big Top, I thought of all the experiences that I had had with Marci. I liked her sexual prowess, but she was becoming so bold that I feared something unpleasant would happen because of her aggressive actions – like pregnancy. I had to be careful because some time soon, she would be wanting to go all the way with her sexual adventures. Nice thought, but I did not want to face the consequences.

"It's about time! We didn't think that you were going to show up," said Charley. "Is everything o.k.?"

"Everything is fine. Just fine."

"I noticed the lipstick all over your face," said Roger. "Who is the lucky girl?"

"Well, now let me see. Among the three of them, I am not sure which one was wearing the lipstick," I said jokingly.

"A foursome, huh?" said Manny. "I wouldn't know how to navigate through that many females. I have trouble with just one."

"In a threesome, foursome or more, I would imagine that I was in a candy store. I would go for the tastiest ones first and then continue until the last morsel," I said. "You might not make it through all of them in one evening, but you could always save the rest for another day."

"Have you seen Miss Goodman lately?" asked Charley. "That woman is getting more beautiful by the week. Every time that I see her, my hormones go into overdrive."

I had to be careful when Miss Goodman was the subject of a conversation.

"No, I haven't seen her for a while," I said. "I certainly have my dreams and fantasies about her. But you guys know that none of us would ever stand a chance with her. All we can do is dream."

"Or as the Everly Brothers said in their song, "All I Have to do is Dream," said Roger.

"Why did they have to talk about Miss Goodman?" I thought. "Now she will be on my mind for the rest of the evening."

Although I knew that Miss Goodman was off limits for more than one reason, I yearned to see her. She did say that if I got lonely I could go to her house. But what if she was joking and teasing me? She sounded sincere and I believed her when she said she also got lonely. I must be bold and brave enough to find out. Should I go to her house tonight or wait patiently for another evening?

I started walking in the direction of her house.

Chapter 16

"Love sought is good, but given unsought is better."
Shakespeare

As I approached her house, I was becoming nervous. Although the evening was cool, I began to perspire and my heart raced as I imagined that I would be indignantly rejected by her. I stepped upon the porch and I could hear Perry Como singing the theme song of his television show. I had lost track of time; I did not know if the show was beginning or ending. Nervously, I knocked on the door. I was stunned when she opened it.

She was dressed in a pair of short-shorts and a blouse that was unbuttoned and tied at the waist. Her legs were perfectly shaped and looked like a movie star's. I could see traces of a black bra from a small opening in her blouse. She looked at me and smiled.

"I didn't expect to see you tonight."

"I had nothing to do, so I thought that I would just stop by and see you briefly."

"Me neither. Would you like to come in and watch television with me? I was just getting ready to pop some corn and have an RC."

"Yes, that would be nice. I never get to watch much television. I'm always too busy."

"Sit on the couch, and I will be right with you."

Her house was a typical one for the area. It was a small, four-room home with two bedrooms, a kitchen-dining room area, and a full bath. Her tastes in home decoration were evident; the walls, carpet, and furniture matched perfectly in color and placement. It looked as though she had the assistance of a professional decorator but I somehow knew that it was her touches throughout the house.

"Finally! The popcorn is ready. Do you want me to change channels or would you prefer to watch Perry Como?"

I really was not interested in Perry Como or any other show. Being with Miss

Goodman suited me fine. I wanted to start a conversation – any conversation with her that she might be interested in.

"This is one of the nicest homes that I have ever seen in Cumberland, Miss Goodman. I just love it."

"Please call me Leslie when we are alone. I am an informal person. Would you want me to call you Mr. White?"

"Absolutely not! That would be awkward for me."

"Now you know how I feel," she said laughing.

After we finished the popcorn and drinks, I watched as she stood to take the popcorn bowl and empty RC bottles into the kitchen and for the first time I got a good look at her from the rear. Her body was solid; she was definitely exercising regularly as evidenced by the tone of her arms, legs, and buttocks. She walked with a swagger in an inadvertent teasing manner. She was every male's dream of both beauty and physical perfection and I desired her in every way.

"That popcorn was really good, don't you think?" she asked as she re-entered the room. "I cannot watch television without popcorn. I crave it as much as I do when I am watching a movie at the Corlee."

"I will remember that the next time that you come to the Corlee. I get popcorn free while I am working."

She sat down on the couch close to me. I could smell her perfume which she apparently had just applied; I did not smell it when I arrived. I was hoping that she had applied it especially for me.

After the Perry Como show, she switched the channel to "Lawrence Welk's Dodge Dance Party."

"I like this show. I love the music, don't you?"

"Yes, I do. I love all types of music. Everything from Country to Pop."

As I said this, she laid her head on my shoulder. Again, I did not know what to do. My movements became frozen; I feared that if I moved she would lift her head from my shoulder. I felt awkward and did not know what to do with my arms and hands.

"If it would make you more comfortable, you may put your arm around me if you wish. You need not be shy."

I put my arm around her and she made a small sigh as though she enjoyed it.

"I must make a confession," I said. "I have been wanting to do this for the longest time, but I was afraid that you might be offended."

"Not at all, I love to sit like this when talking or watching a movie or TV with you. You must promise, though, that you will never let anyone know about this. I could get into a lot of trouble with the school."

"But you are not my teacher this year. You have my word, though, that I will tell no one, not even my closest friends."

"Then we have an understanding," she said.

As I was enjoying every minute while her head was resting on my shoulder, I did not know what else she expected me to do. I thought that I would test her by brushing my hand against her breast. I lifted my arm to scratch my head and as I put my arm around her again, I briefly touched her breast and quickly withdrew it.

"Oh, I am sorry," I said.

"That is quite all right," she said. "Someday soon."

What did she mean by "someday soon"? I could not ask her, but I began to get excited. Was she teasing me again or was this a harbinger of things to come?

At the end of the show, she stood up and stretched her body in ways that was designed to tease me even more, or at least I thought it was. I enjoyed watching every movement of her body; I knew, though, that the evening was ending and she was ready for me to leave.

She escorted me to the door. I turned to say good night; she put her arms around me and hugged me tightly. She withdrew slightly, looked into my eyes and unexpectedly kissed me lightly on the lips. I almost fell over with excitement. I felt as though this goddess from Mt. Olympus was allowing one of her minions to experience what true love was really like. I almost swooned over the excitement. I wanted more, but I knew that I had to leave.

"Good night," she said. "See you soon."

"I really enjoyed myself. Drop by the Corlee anytime. You know that you are always welcome."

"I will do that," she said.

I did not sleep that night. I was restless and my brain was in overdrive trying to make sense of the evening. Leslie was in my every thought; I was fearful that our relationship, whatever it was or would become, would crash and leave me an emotional wreck.

When I arose the next morning, I felt so groggy that I was concerned that I would fall asleep at work. I had to have company to keep me awake, so I asked Judy to meet me at the Corlee at noon to spend the day with me. I was happy to see her; we had a great afternoon just talking and reminiscing.

The Christmas season of 1957 and New Year's Day passed quickly. Almost everyone was ready to start the second semester and the new year of 1958. This was going to be another pivotal year for me. I would get my driver's license and car in six months, giving me new freedoms and new places to explore.

The halls were filled with smiling students conversing and laughing. Lockers could be heard opening and closing and everyone was scurrying about to locate friends that they had not been seen for a couple of weeks. Manny, Charley, Roger and I were on our way to our classrooms.

"I don't know why I have to take English," said Manny. "I speak it well enough for everyone to understand me. I don't need to know what a noun, pronoun, verb, or object is; it is not that important to me. And I don't like to read books that no one understands but geniuses."

"Reading books expands your mind," I said. "They offer experiences that you could never find otherwise."

"Manny has so much in that head of his about automobiles that he doesn't have any more room to spare," quipped Roger.

"Well, could Einstein, Shakespeare, or Benjamin Franklin repair cars?" asked Manny.

"I do know that neither Shakespeare nor Benjamin Franklin could repair a car because it hadn't been invented yet," I said. "I really don't know about Einstein. I think that he was too busy working on the Unified Field Theory to worry about auto repair."

"What kind of field?" asked Manny, "corn, potato, or what?"

"You should read and find out for yourself, Manny," said Charley.

"I will let the geniuses take care of those types of problems," said Manny. "I have enough to worry about as it is."

We studied and worked hard to complete our first year of high school. I was pleased that throughout the year I was on the honor roll despite my working hours. When the last bell rang, I hurried outside of the building to wait for my friends. I had a good feeling that this would be the best summer break that I ever had.

Chapter 17

"License my roving hands, and let them go before, behind, between,
above, below."
John Donne

On May 28th, I turned 16 sixteen years old, a date that was special to me; it was time to obtain my driver's license.

Within the first week of June, I took my written exam. Once I received my learner's permit, my dad taught me to drive within a short period of time. Within two weeks, I took the driver's test and passed it with high praise from the Kentucky State Police officer who was the examiner.

Figure 14. Me at sixteen.

I immediately began to search for a used car that would be reliable and attractive. I settled for a 1953 Chevy Bel Air Coupe with "three on the tree," or a standard shift three speed transmission with

169

the gear lever on the steering column. The car was only five years old; it was yellow with a brown top that stood out because of its bright color. As I drove it home, I got thumbs up from my friends and neighbors.

I wanted to cruise the streets of Cumberland, Benham, and Lynch to show off my new ride. Gasoline at the time cost 23¢ a gallon. The car got about 25 miles per gallon of gas, which meant that I could travel 100 miles on four gallons at a cost of 92¢. That was a lot of cruising for less than a dollar.

Figure 15. 1953 Chevy Bel Air Coupe. Identical to the one that I owned at 16.

The first day that I took possession of the car, I cruised almost every street in Cumberland, Benham, and Lynch over and over again. The dusty gravel road on Cloverlick was also traveled many times. My car would later become a familiar fixture for miles around; it was the only one that I knew of in the Tri-City area with its color scheme.

My friends wanted to name the car, a tradition among us greasers. We sat around for some time attempting to give it an appropriate name that would reflect our styles and personalities.

"How about the 'Yellow Hornet'? I always liked the radio show the 'Green Hornet.' The name would fit the color of the car," said Roger.

"Too copy-cat for me," I said. "I want something original."

"How about the 'Studmobile'? That would describe both the car and its occupants," said Charley.

"I don't know," I said. "We would have a difficult time picking up chicks at their house with a name like that. Can you imagine a father and mother allowing their daughter to go cruising in a car with a name like the 'Studmobile'?"

"Point taken," said Charley.

Many names were offered, but the one that we chose was Manny's suggestion, of all people.

"Why don't we call it 'Peggy Sue'?" he said. "Every mother wants their daughters to be a 'Peggy Sue'. It is also a great song by Buddy Holly."

"Manny, that is brilliant," I said. "You are the next....

"Don't go telling me about another thousand year-old cool cat again," he said. "I don't want to hear it."

"O.k., let's go cruising," I said.

And we cruised, and cruised, and....

After I drove the guys' home, I washed and cleaned the car thoroughly. I was now ready to show the girls my new ride. "But who would be the first?" I thought.

I drove to Judy's house, and as soon as I parked on the side of the road, she ran to the car excited and kept saying, "Nice, very nice! Are you going to take me for a ride?"

"How about going to the Pine View this evening and order our food from the car?" I said. "I have always wanted to that."

"I would love it," she said. "Is 7:30 o.k. with you?"

"Fine, I will pick you up then."

I went home and prepared for the evening. I bathed for the second time that day, donned a pair of jeans and my favorite shirt with a large collar. I rolled up the cuffs of the jeans and added an extra splash of shave lotion. I then spent about ten minutes grooming my hair, which got most of the attention while preparing for a date. An extra dab of Brylcream assured a high sheen to my black hair, and I combed every inch of it many times over. I stood in front of the mirror for a couple of minutes after combing it and gave myself thumbs up. Judy would approve, I thought.

I then drove proudly through town to pick her up.

We drove to the Pine View, and I flashed my lights to let the carhops know that we wanted food service at my car. Judy was sitting close to me as though she wanted everyone inside the restaurant to notice both of us. And they did.

The service was quick and the food seemed to taste better in the car. Judy enjoyed it as much as I did.

"I have never had food delivered to me in a car before," she said. "This is a lot of fun."

"Would you like to go somewhere else after we finish eating?"

"Yes, and I am willing to go wherever you want to as long as I get home by 11:00."

We left the Pine View after our meal and drove to Cloverlick. There were many spots on the side of the road to park, but I chose the place where we had the party and bonfire. It was a favorite site to take a date; when darkness fell on the moonless night, it was difficult to see objects at close range. That meant that we could not been seen by a passerby.

"I love this place. It is so peaceful and quiet," said Judy.

"Me, too. And it is so private."

I turned the car radio on and received a station playing rock and roll music. The DJ was playing Billboard's chart of the top 100 hits in descending order. Rock and roll music was crowding the charts that were formerly occupied by singers such as Dean Martin, Frank Sinatra, Patti Page, Doris Day, Teresa Brewer, and many other great pop stars of the day. It was a perfect night for a date with someone like Judy and the music added to the ambience of the evening. I liked her a lot and as I had become to know more about her, I liked her even more.

Judy moved in the direction of the passenger door and tugged at my arm to signal that she wanted me to move close to her and out of the way of the steering wheel. I moved over and put my arm around her and held her in a tight hug. She kissed me lightly on the lips, my cheeks, and forehead while running her fingers through my hair.

She then gave me a passionate kiss that was similar to the way that Marci would kiss me.

"Wow! You are a great kisser. Could you do that for the rest of the evening," I said jokingly.

"Only if you want me to."

"Silly girl. I certainly want you to. I could do this for the rest of eternity."

She gave me a quizzical look. I knew that there was something that she wanted to ask me but she was, perhaps, reluctant to because of the answer that I might give her.

"If I asked you to do the same to me that you did to Marci, what exactly would you do?" she asked.

"I don't know what you mean. What exactly did she tell you that we did?"

"Well, she really didn't say much of anything that went on with the two of you."

"It was really nothing much. There might have been a little fondling, but nothing beyond that."

"Did you like it?"

"Of course I did! As far as I know, she loved it, too, but I do not know how a girl would normally feel under those circumstances."

"Would you do it with me?"

"Do what? There is really nothing of consequence to do."

"Well, whatever you did."

"Let's switch places."

"Why?" she asked

"Because I'm right handed. I was always uncomfortable sitting on the left side when kissing. You want me to do this, don't you?" as I reached for her breasts.

I held her into my arms and kissed her until both of us were breathing rapidly from the excitement. She squeezed my hand against her breast and sighed.

"What else did you do?"

"I can't tell you that, Judy. I respect her privacy. Would you want me to let

177

everyone know what happens between you and me on a date?"

"No! I see what you mean."

"Let's just enjoy what we are doing and forget about Marci," I said.

"O.k.," she said. "And could you do that again please? Yes, right there!"

What happened between Marci and me was spreading all over Cumberland, even though nothing really happened. The story changes daily as it spreads from one person to another. Soon I will be a prolific lover as Casanova was by way of rumor only. I liked it in an odd sort of way. Maybe my reputation will be enhanced because of the rumors representing the good things that allegedly happen, or harmed by the things that might prevent parents from letting their daughters date me by the alleged bad ones.

Chapter 18

"The greatest thing in this world is not so much where we stand as
in what direction we are moving."
Johann Wolfgang von Goethe

The summer of 1958 was a memorable one. Receiving my driver's license and purchasing a car were goals that were brought to fruition, I had a good job, and I was successful in high school. My car expanded my circle of friends to include Lynch and the surrounding areas of Cumberland that were not available to me previously.

The summer seemed to fade fast; I was preparing for my sophomore year in school. That year I took courses in Chemistry, Biology and Algebra, in addition to two other subjects that would keep me busy for the year. I took advantage of study hall so that I would not have to spend all of my evenings studying; I needed time for social interaction which was one of my most basic wants and needs.

Before the start of school, Manny, Charley, Roger, and I decided take a trip to

Virginia to see an old friend, Donny Salyers, who had moved there many years prior. It was so far down into the state that we had to arrange for overnight accommodations. Donny recommended a motel that was the cheapest that he could find for us. I called and reserved two rooms and gave them the arrival date.

We loaded what little luggage that we had into the Chevy the evening before departure so that we could get an early start the next morning. We were excited and anxious for morning to come.

"I have never been that far down into Virginia, so everything that I see will be new to me," said Roger.

"Me, too! I heard that those Virginia girls are beautiful and ready," said Manny.

"Ready for what?" asked Charley.

"Ready for love," said Manny.

"Girls are the same everywhere, Manny. They will be no different than the ones in Cumberland who think that you are a pervert," said Charley.

"If that is true, then I will look for the bad girl types. I have a thing for them anyway," said Manny.

The next morning we loaded a few more personal items into the car. I turned the key to start the car; it gave a slow growl and was reluctant to start. After three tries, the engine started and we were on our way to Roanoke, which was close to where Donny's family lived. After passing through Roanoke, we searched for, but could not find, the road leading to our destination.

Our search was complicated as the sky darkened and it began to rain heavily. Rather than continue, we stopped at a diner and ordered a late lunch. We relaxed until the storm abated and asked the waitress for directions.

"Could you direct us to Spurlock Road?" I asked.

"Never heard of it, honey," she said. "The closest thing that comes to that is Sherlock Road, but I don't think that anyone lives on it."

"Do you know of a family by the name of Salyers?" I asked.

"Never heard of them. I know just about everyone living within a five mile radius of this restaurant, but I do not recall anyone by that name," she said.

"I would suggest that we continue in the direction that we were going and take our chances," said Roger. "If we do not find Spurlock Road within twenty miles, we will regroup."

Reluctantly, I took Roger's advice and drove in the direction that we were previously headed. We traveled about fifteen more miles and spotted a barn. There were many cars parked around it. We could hear the sounds of a banjo, guitar, fiddle, and slap bass playing Bluegrass music. We parked and went into the barn. There were approximately one hundred people dancing, talking, drinking, and having a wonderful time.

"Come on in and join us," said an older man dressed in bib overalls. "It only costs a buck for admission."

"Actually, we were heading to Spurlock Road. Could you direct us to it?" I asked.

"Never heard of it," he said. "Does anyone here know where Spurlock Road is?" he asked the crowd.

"No," everyone said in unison.

"It is getting late," I said to the guys. "Unfortunately, we are also not going to find our motel which is supposed to be close to Spurlock Road. What do you want to do?"

"I want to stay here and party with these people," said Manny. "Looks like they are having a lot of fun."

"We are in agreement," said Roger and Charley. "This looks like the place to be right now."

We each paid the one dollar admission charge and went into the barn.

"Want a drink?" a man asked who appeared to be the owner of the barn. "Drinks are only fifty cents. It is some of the best stuff in the county."

"Sure, we'll have one," said Charley.

The man brought four drinks in plastic cups.

"This will set you free," said the man whom everyone was calling Hoss.

I put the cup to my mouth and took a large sip. I swallowed the contents and as I did, a fire was kindled inside my whole body. I should have known that it was moonshine. My breath left me momentarily, and I felt that the fire in my throat and stomach would never subside.

"Pretty good stuff, huh?" said Hoss.

"It is powerful," I said. "My car would probably run on this stuff. This is the first time that I ever tasted moonshine."

After we emptied our cups of the White Lightning, we were feeling good. As the music played, four unaccompanied girls about our age asked us to dance.

"You guys go ahead," I said. "I am going to sit this one out."

"You don't want to dance with me?" asked one of the girls.

"I am not a good dancer."

"Do you want to go outside for a while? Maybe we can find something to do out there."

"Sure, I need some fresh air after that drink."

We went outside and she directed me toward the rear of the barn.

"So you're lost, huh? Where are you from?"

"Cumberland, Kentucky," I said. "On the other side of Black Mountain."

"I have never been there myself. I am stuck in this area and I never get a chance to travel. I am so happy that you guys came here tonight. I keep seeing the same people over and over and they are so boring. We don't see many strangers in these parts. They never stay more than a couple of days and they leave. Are you leaving soon?"

"Yes, when my friends are ready."

"Why don't you stay here for the night? When it gets dark, you will never find your way out of here."

"Where would we stay?"

"Right here in the barn. The best place to sleep is in the hayloft. Hoss will accommodate you and your friends."

"I will ask him later. I believe that you are right. I do not think that it is wise to leave tonight."

"I have already talked to him. He said that it would be fine if you and your friends would like to spend the night in the barn. The girls and I will keep you company if you want us to."

"That could get you into trouble. I don't think that it would be a good idea."

"We will see," she said.

We talked to Hoss about the evenings arrangements. He agreed that we could sleep in the hayloft – for two bucks apiece. That was steep for a night in the hayloft, but we did not have much choice.

We were each supplied with two blankets that were old and smelled like horses, but we had no other choice. I had never slept in a barn before, and I was not looking forward to it.

When the music stopped and the partygoers left, it was approaching 11:00 and we were getting tired. We climbed the ladder into the hayloft with our blankets and searched for a comfortable place to sleep. The hayloft was large; the bales of hay were scattered and stacked in twos, so privacy was easy to find for each of us. For safety and security, we lifted the ladder into the hayloft.

Within twenty minutes, we heard sounds from below. It was the girls that we met earlier. There was another girl with them who was about two years older than the others.

"May we come up?" asked the older girl. "We can party all night long. I have drinks."

I whispered as low as I could.

"Look, guys, we had better not let them up here. I know at least one of them is Hoss' daughter. I do not want to face the consequences if he sees her with us."

"I say that we party," said Manny. "We came to Virginia for a good time; this is our opportunity."

"We agree," said Roger and Charley.

Roger and Charley lowered the ladder.

"Come on up, girls," said Manny. "We are ready for you."

The older girl had a quart size Mason jar filled with moonshine which she passed around to each of us. We took small sips from the jar until we drank one-half of its contents.

"This stuff is powerful. I am feeling woozy," said Manny. "I think that I am going to sleep now."

Each of us began to feel as Manny did; none of us remembered much of what happened before we went to sleep, but we did remember that the girls had taken their clothes off and were lying next to us just before we lost consciousness. I also remembered a tug at my pants close to my belt line and the older girl handing me a condom. What happened after that will forever remain a mystery.

We awakened the following morning at 8:00 with massive headaches. I was so sick that I vomited on the nearest bale of hay that I could find. The others did the same shortly thereafter. I wondered which farm animals would be the ones that would eat from those bales, a thought so sickening that I vomited again.

"We must leave this place as quickly as we can," I said. "I am concerned that Hoss will find out that those girls were up here with us. I certainly do not want a confrontation with him."

When we descended the ladder, I opened the barn door and looked in all directions.

"Come on guys, everything is clear. Let's get out of here fast," I said.

The car was only steps away from us; I ran and unlocked the doors as quickly as I could. I turned the key to the start position and the car hesitated. After three more tries it started. I put the car into low gear, stepped hard on the accelerator pedal, and spun the wheels as I released the clutch. We were on the road at a relatively high speed; as the barn faded into the distance, I slowed down and breathed a sigh of relief.

"I will never do that again," I said. "Let's find a place to eat. I am hungry."

A few miles down the road, we stopped at a combination grocery store, gas station, and restaurant. Each of us ordered a huge breakfast of eggs, country ham, biscuits, and gravy. The waitress watched as we downed the food rapidly.

"You boys sure were hungry," she said as she placed our checks on the table. "You all come back soon."

"That's not likely," said Roger as the waitress walked out of hearing range. "I never want to see this place again."

We went to the register to pay our checks. I reached into my back pocket and discovered that my wallet was missing.

"Hey, those girls stole my wallet," I said.

"Mine was stolen, too," said Manny.

Charley and Roger reached into their back pockets and also discovered theirs missing.

"What are we going to do?" asked Manny. "We have no money to pay our checks."

"One thing that I never do is carry a lot of cash on me in the event that I lose my wallet," I said. "I have most of it in one of my bags in the trunk of the car."

I opened the trunk of the car and obtained enough money from my bag to pay for our meals, a tank of gas, and four RCs to drink on the way home. Everyone smiled as we headed in the direction of Cumberland.

I still do not know exactly where Donny lived in Virginia, and I would never try to find my way there again.

And we did not dare to go back to inquire about our wallets. We decided to write them off as a valuable lesson learned.

Chapter 19

"My sexual preference is often."
Anonymous

When we arrived in Cumberland, I took Roger, Manny, and Charley home and drove to the Big Top late that afternoon. It felt good to be at a familiar place where the food was good and the waitresses were always friendly.

"I haven't seen you for a while," said Patsy. "You just missed Marci, Diana, and Judy. They were all here together."

"I am here for a meal and relaxation. I wouldn't know how to handle three girls right now," I said jokingly. "One is sometimes too much for me."

"Miss Goodman was here last night and asked me if I had seen you lately. She was joking about a ride in your new car that you had promised her."

"I must see her," I thought. "But I am reluctant to make the first move. Maybe we will have a chance meeting soon."

"My shift is over in an hour if you want to do something this afternoon. I would also like to ride in your new car."

"Sure. I have nothing but time for the rest of the day and evening. I will sit here and wait for you."

"What am I going to do for an hour to keep me occupied?" I thought. "I can only eat and drink so much over the next hour."

The Big Top was practically empty except for two elderly couples who were complaining about their arthritis, their latest operations and what the world was coming to with the misbehavior of young people.

"It seems that all teenagers are interested in is Rock and Roll music and sex these days," said one of the women.

"If I remember correctly, Edna, you were no different when you were younger. You went nuts every time that a Frank Sinatra or Bing Crosby record was played on the radio," said her husband Roy. "Sure, the dancing was different, but I don't think there has been that much of a change in young people over the years. They don't dress the way we did, but I don't believe that you would really want to wear the fashions that you wore when you were a teenager, would you?"

"No, I wouldn't," said Edna. "The dresses were so long that they dragged on the ground behind me. Heaven forbid if the girls had to dress that way today."

"We were not as loose with our bodies as girls are today," said Mabel. "Have you heard about that girl Diana Smith? I hear that she is having sex with Roger Sherwood. She is way too young to be bedded by that leather jacket wearing delinquent."

Roger and Diana? He had not told me that he was dating her, but that was none of my business. I decided that I would not ask him about it. I do not tell him about my love life, so why should he tell me about his.

"Ready to go?" asked Patsy. "They are letting me off a little early. There is not that much business today."

"Where would you like to go? Cincinnati, Indianapolis, or Miami?"

"How about Lynch," she said smiling.

As we entered the car, she moved over to the center of the seat.

"You don't currently have a steady girlfriend, do you? I wouldn't want anyone to get angry with me for sitting so close to you."

"You are safe. But in the event that one of the girls that I dated in the past gets angry, I have a wheel wrench that you can use to fend them off with," I said with a smile.

When we arrived in Lynch, Patsy asked me to take a street that I had never traveled before next to Lynch High School.

"What street is this?"

"Gap Branch. I have a friend that I would like to see briefly. You can wait in the car. It is the house close to the curve. I will bring her out to meet you later."

I parked the car on the opposite side of the street. Patsy ran across the street as though she was in a hurry. Five minutes later she returned with her friend.

"This is Mary Ann Searcy, my long-time friend."

When she introduced me to her I could not believe the beauty of the girl standing in front of me. Her hair was black, she was about two inches shorter than me and resembled Annette Funicello, my dream date. Her hair was styled exactly like Annette's, her build was also similar, and she spoke in one of the sexiest voices that I had ever heard. She obviously made every effort to mimic Annette's looks and mannerisms. I could sit and admire her all day, but I would never stand a chance with this gorgeous creature.

"Nice to meet you," I said nervously. "I would bet that many have compared you to Annette Funicello."

"Yes, I have heard that. It is a nice compliment and it flatters me, but I have my own personality."

"Patsy said that you are about to begin your sophomore year in high school. I am, too. I'll bet that you are looking forward to it."

"Yes, I am. I love school. I have a heavy schedule this year, but I'll handle it well."

Figure 16. Annette Funicello.

"Patsy also said that you work at the Corlee and that you can get anyone in free. Maybe you can get me in free sometime."

"Any time that you want to. Just be there at noon on a Saturday or Sunday."

"I will keep that in mind. I understand that I can also sit in the balcony. I have never been in the balcony."

"Just let me know, and I will arrange it. I would love to see you there."

"I must go now," said Patsy with a cold stare toward Mary Ann. "I have a lot to do when I get home."

Patsy was obviously jealous of Mary Ann and I could understand why. I made the mistake of leaving her out of the conversation, but I was totally enthralled by Mary Ann's looks and personality.

Patsy entered the car and moved close to me. It was apparent that she wanted Mary Ann to notice her.

"I think that you really like her," said Patsy as we drove off.

"Yes, I do," I said. "Indeed I do."

After driving Patsy home, I wanted to be alone. I drove to Cloverlick, pulled to the side of the road, and turned on the car radio. As I listened, thoughts of Mary Ann rushed through my head. Since I knew nothing about her, I concluded that it was her physical beauty only that attracted me to her. I knew that I should not judge her for that reason alone, so I decided that I would forget her. What chance would I have anyway? As I was thinking of her, I laid my head back on the seat and went into a deep, restful, and dreamless sleep.

I awoke refreshed from a two hour nap, started the car, and headed in the direction of Leslie Goodman's house.

As I approached the front door, I heard the sound of her record player. The recording was "It's Only Make Believe" by Conway Twitty, a song that I was beginning to love for its message. Before I knocked on the door, she opened it and smiled.

"Well, look who's here. I finally get to see your new car," she said. "Do I get a ride?"

"Now?" I asked.

"Sure, why not? It is getting dark; this is a good time to go. I can't be seen for obvious reasons."

"Where to, my lady," I said jokingly.

"Anywhere that there are not a lot of people. Just being cautious."

"I know a place in Gilley Holler where no would will be travelling at this time. It is a perfect place next to a cemetery."

"Then the cemetery it will be," she said with a hearty laugh.

When we arrived, I turned the headlights off. It was so dark that I could see her face only faintly.

"Wow, I have never been in a place this dark before. It is kind of scary, but I have confidence that you will protect me from the ghosts and boogeymen."

I turned the car radio on to a station that was playing Billboard's top 100 songs. The small amount of light coming from the radio pierced the darkness that surrounded us. I could now see Leslie's facial features clearly.

"Do you mind if move over toward you?"

"Not at all. I would like that."

"If you like, you may put your arm around me. I just want to sit back and listen to that wonderful music."

I placed my arm around her. As if did, she laid her head on my shoulder and gave a small sigh.

"Please understand that I am not being forward with you; as I have said before, I like to be in this position when watching TV, at the movies, or listening to music. It is such a relaxing feeling."

"I understand. I like to be in this position, too. It gives me a lot of pleasure just being with you."

"You know how to make a girl feel good," she said with a chuckle. "How would you define pleasure? I ask you this from a teacher's point of view."

"I think that it is a relative term just as the word love is. If you ask me what water was made of, I could easily define it chemically as two atoms of hydrogen and one atom of oxygen; it cannot be defined accurately in any other way. But if you ask a group of people what love or pleasure is, each person will give you a completely different answer. Essentially, there is no concrete definition for the words love and pleasure, only emotional attempts at one."

"I agree. What are your pleasures?"

"My family, good food, my car, my friends, etc. I find pleasure in all of them and many other things."

"What about sexual pleasure? Do you like that?"

"Sure, I do. But I have not had sex in the way that it is done traditionally. By that, I mean that I have never penetrated a woman."

She looked at me, smiled, and stared into my eyes. I was so nervous that I began to perspire.

"You seem so nervous. If you are uncomfortable by being here with me, we can leave."

"Oh, not at all. It is just that you are so beautiful that I....."

She put her hand on my face and kissed me. My whole body trembled. I began to perspire profusely; I was getting so excited that my mind went totally blank.

"Is that what you wanted to do?"

"Ye...yes. I have always wanted to."

I became bolder and put both of my arms around her and gave her a passionate kiss.

"That was really nice," she said. "It was more than I expected; I didn't know that things would go this far. I hope that you will not think of me any differently."

"My feelings for you will never change. When I am with you, I feel like I am dreaming. I would like to kiss you all night."

"I have all night. If I go home, I would be alone and bored. Come here! I forgot to give you a gift on your birthday. Now show me what you would REALLY like to do to me."

That night, I had my first sexual experience with an older woman, and my former teacher, whose passion seemed limitless. I was lost for words to describe it; a comparison could only be made to previous such experiences, which I obviously did not have, as I told her when she asked.

Afterward, we sat in the car for many hours talking, kissing, and cuddling. I was hoping that she would remain with me all evening, but I knew that it would not happen when she looked at her watch.

"Tonight has been a special night for me, but it has its drawbacks," said Leslie. "You have to promise me that you will tell no one about this; I would be fired immediately if there was even a hint that I went on a date with you."

"You don't have to worry about that. I will forever keep our secret and I am good at that. I would never want to see you in trouble with anyone, especially the school board."

"Just remember that. And me!" she said as she was combing her hair.

"How could I ever forget you? You made my evening one of the most exciting ever."

As I started the car, she moved back toward the passenger door. I could tell that she was fearful of being seen.

"You can hunker down as we get close to Cumberland. No one will be able to see you."

"When you get close to my house, would you please let me out of the car at the end of my street? You know how neighbors will talk."

"I sure will," I said as I drove out of Gilly Holler and onto Cloverlick road leading to Cumberland.

Leslie was silent during the drive home. I glanced at her. It appeared that she was in deep thought.

"Are you o.k.?" I asked.

"Yes, I am fine. Did you think that I was too forward with you this evening? I don't want you to think that I do this often.

Actually you are the first person that I have been with in a long time."

"No, I enjoyed being with you. I was hopeful that the evening would turn out the way it did. I have thought of you a lot. You have always been my fantasy date."

She looked at me and smiled.

"I was hoping that you would say something like that. Tonight was a night that both of us will probably long remember."

"If you only knew," I thought. "If you only knew."

Chapter 20

"Never give up on someone you can't go a day without thinking about."
Anonymous

On the first day of school, I was so happy when I walked through those doors to CHS. I was now a sophomore, as were my friends Roger, Charley, and Manny. The first one that I spotted that morning was Roger who was arm-in-arm with Diana. Charley and Manny were running to greet us.

"Congratulations to you and Roger," I said to Diana. "You two make a fine looking couple."

"Yeah," said Charley. "You are one lucky man, Roger."

"Yes, you are," said Manny. "You are dating a girl who has more class than you do, she's smarter, and she is far better looking than you deserve."

Diana laughed loudly.

"That is exactly what I told him. He is a lucky man. I suppose that I can tolerate him until someone like you comes along Manny," she said jokingly.

"Hey! Where have you been girl? In a convent? I have been available all along. All that you would have to do is look at me and flash those beautiful sexy eyes, and I would be yours forever," said Manny

"Too late now," said Diana with a chuckle. "Maybe we will meet in fantasyland someday."

"I belong in fantasyland," said Manny. "Fantasies are all that I have to cling to now."

"There goes the bell, see you guys later," I said. "Maybe we could all meet after school and do some cruising."

"I won't be able to," said Roger. "I am going to Diana's house tonight. Maybe another day."

Diana lowered her head when Roger said "maybe another day." I took that to mean that she disapproved of Roger's friendship with me for some reason. But that was Roger's decision; I never interceded in such conflicts.

As expected, Chemistry and Biology took a lot of study. Classes were on Mondays, Wednesdays, and Fridays, with labs on Tuesdays and Thursdays. Of all the classes that I had, I loved lab work the most. Performing experiments and being able to predict the outcomes of them were exciting. But to some, the physical and natural sciences were punishments handed to them by evil, scheming teachers to amuse themselves by gleefully watching their students being tortured in the classroom and laboratory.

In our lab work, the teacher paired us up to work together on experiments and biological observations. It was helpful to have someone next to you when there were procedural questions, especially in the dissection of animals. I had an excellent biology lab partner, Jill Hall, in high school who was also my lab partner in our freshmen year in college. We learned a lot from each other's work, and I remember her fondly.

I was also becoming more interested in Literary Arts. Nineteenth century English and Russian literature became my favorites. I was in awe of the likes of Leo Tolstoy, Fyodor Dostoevsky, Charles Dickens, Emily and Charlotte Bronte, and far too many more authors to list. Today, I have hundreds of such books on my Kindle and I have read many of them numerous times like Dostoevsky's "Crime and Punishment," and Tolstoy's trilogy of "Childhood," "Boyhood," and "Youth." Charles Dickens works were fascinating; he wrote of the abject poverty, injustices and cruelty of 19th Century England in his novels. Although most of his works were fiction, his graphic look at life of that era was based on fact.

Not long after school started, I discovered that my workload at two theaters was too much for me. I gave my resignation to the manager of the Auburn Drive-In but decided to continue to work at the Corlee. It was a relief to have evenings off on Friday, Saturday, and Sunday; it gave me more time to study and maintain my social life.

With my new-found freedom, I decided to attend the Auburn Drive-In on Saturday night for the first time in my own car. It was difficult to choose who would accompany me. Would it be Marci, Judy, Patsy, or...

"Wait a minute," I thought. "I am going to drive to Gap Branch and ask Mary Ann Searcy if she would like to go. I knew that she would probably refuse, but if she did, at least I would know that I tried."

Driving through Benham, I was beginning to have second thoughts. I met Mary Ann only briefly before. She does not know me and I really did not know her. She probably has more date requests than she can deal with, and I would be just one of many in pursuit of her.

As I was thinking of all the negatives, I suddenly found myself close to Gap Branch. With some trepidation, I turned right and continued to her house. As I exited the car, I was more nervous than ever, but I managed to finally knock on the door. Mary Ann greeted me almost instantly.

"I am sorry that I came unannounced. I took a chance that you would be home. I would be honored if you would go with me to the Auburn Drive-In this evening."

"This is a short notice, but I am happy that you asked me out. I wondered if I would ever see you again. I would love to go, but I would have to get permission from my parents. Wait here for a moment."

She went into the house and closed the door. I was sure that this was going to be a waste of my time and hers. Her parents are not going to give her permission to go the Drive-In with someone that they had never met. I began to perspire anticipating her answer.

She opened the door. There was a smile on her face. I waited for a "sorry, not tonight; maybe some other time" answer.

"Come in and meet my parents. And don't worry, they won't bite you. I promise."

Mary Ann's mother, Cindy, resembled her in every way. She was in her mid-thirties, but looked ten years younger. Her physique was also close to that of her daughters. She was beautiful and seemed humble and kind.

"I understand that you met my daughter only once. She said that you had a job at the Corlee Theater and that you are a sophomore at Cumberland High School. I admire that in a young man," she said.

"Yes. I had to resign my job at the Auburn. Working two jobs and attending school was too much for me. Working at the Corlee part-time is ideal for my situation."

Her dad did not speak. He shook his head in agreement at everything that Mrs. Searcy said.

We talked for about thirty minutes. Mrs. Searcy asked enough questions to get a complete history on me and my family including: where I lived, what my dad did for a living, how many siblings I had, and information on other family members. When I mentioned my mother's maiden name, Creech, she became more attentive.

"Are you related to any of the Creech's (and there were many) who own businesses in Cumberland?" she asked.

"All of them, although some are distant relatives."

"When would you pick my daughter up and when would you bring her home?"

"About 7:30. I would have her home at any time that you wish."

"Fine. You be here at 7:30 and have her home by midnight, and not a minute later."

I was overjoyed that Mary Ann would actually be my date for the evening. I thanked her mother and father profusely and I promised to take care of their daughter.

Mary Ann walked me to the door.

"See you at 7:30," she said. "And don't be late."

"You can count on it."

On my way home, I went to the Big Top hoping to see Manny and Charley. I knew that Roger would not be there. He would be with Diana. They were kibitzing with the waitresses as usual.

"Where have you been, man?" asked Charley. "We have been looking for you for some time."

"I have been to Lynch to see Mary Ann Searcy."

"You mean Annette Funicello? It's funny, but every time I see her, I think of Frankie Avalon," said Manny.

"You think of Frankie Avalon? Do you dream about him? Would you want a boyfriend that looks like him," asked Charley.

"You are such a wiseacre, Charley. I meant that every time that you see Annette in the movies, Frankie is always by her side singing to her. Why does he waste his time doing that? If I were him, I would just get down to business with that angel with no wings," said Manny.

216

"I think that you would have a better chance with Frankie," said Charley.

"And you would have a better chance with Ma Kettle. That is, if Pa Kettle wouldn't object," said Manny.

"Did you somehow trick her into a date with you?" asked Charley.

"Yes, I am taking her to the Auburn tonight. I even have the official approval of her mother. Eat your heart out guys."

"Wow! Are you going to park in the back row?" asked Manny.

"Only if she wants to. I just hope that she does."

Chapter 21

"Some people grumble that roses have thorns; I am grateful that thorns have roses."
Alphonse Karr

Now that I had a date with Mary Ann, I had a strong urge to impress her. It was my goal to create an atmosphere that would lead to future dates with her. What could I do initially to put a smile on her face?

I stopped at a florist and bought her a dozen roses along with a box of chocolates that I purchased at the drug store. I laid them carefully in the back seat, took a deep breath, and drove toward Lynch.

"It is now or never," I thought.

It was close to 7:30 when I parked in front of the Searcy house. I could see Mary Ann peeking through the front window. She smiled as I stepped upon the porch with the flowers and chocolates.

"That is so sweet of you," she said. "Mom, come look at what Bobby Darrell brought me."

Mrs. Searcy entered the room with a wide smile on her face. She looked as happy as Mary Ann.

"This is a first," Mrs. Searcy said. "No one has ever given flowers OR chocolates to Mary Ann. You two have a good time, and remember that 12:00 is curfew time, Mary Ann."

Mary Ann took one of the roses and we walked out the door toward the car.

"Thanks for the flowers and chocolates. I love them both."

We arrived at the Auburn just before 8:00. I stopped at the ticket booth, and was waved through by the manager. The Auburn was managed by the same family that managed the Corlee, so admission for me and one guest was free.

"Where would you like to park?" I asked. "We have a lot of choices as you can see."

"Where do you usually park?"

"This is the first time that I have been here with my own car, but when I came here many times before with my friends, they would park in the back row. You choose and that is where we will park."

"The back row would be fine with me."

"This is going to be one fine evening," I thought.

When the movie started, Mary Ann moved to the center of seat. I looked at her and she smiled.

"My mother told me that we should not park in the back row. She said that there was a lot of hanky-panky that goes on back here."

"There is, but a lot of couples park back here for privacy so that they can neck. Not all activity is hanky-panky."

I slipped my arm around her without moving too close. I did not want to spoil her evening in any way.

The lights dimmed around the concession stand after the movie started. It was not a good one, but I did not care. I did not think that she did either.

After the first reel of the movie, she moved closer and laid her head on my shoulder.

"I am so happy that I could come with you this evening. I am having such a great time," she said.

"Me, too. I was hoping that we could do this often."

"We will!" she said.

As the evening advanced, she looked up at me and kissed me lightly on the lips. I responded by kissing her forehead, cheeks, and lips. I put both of my arms around her, laid her head back on the seat, and kissed her at length. Her breathing became heavy; she took my hand and placed it on her waist and signaled for me to bring her body close to mine. When she turned on her side, I pulled her close to me and continued to kiss her passionately for about five minutes,

221

after which she gave a little scream of delight and relaxed her hold on me. Her heavy breathing subsided and she looked at me with a wide smile.

"I loved that, and I think that I love you. I wish that we could do this all night, but you know that I have to be home by 12:00. It is now 11:30."

"Unfortunately, time is not on our side tonight. I know that we must leave so that you will be home on time. I will never forget this evening and I hope that we can repeat it soon. That is, if you are so inclined."

"I am all for it."

"If we get home a little early, we can sit in the car until midnight. We will use our time up to the last minute," she said.

On the way to Lynch, she kept her head on my shoulder. She took her hand and softly touched my cheek and then patted me on the opposite shoulder. I pulled to the side of the road in a private spot just before we arrived at her house. I did not want to leave her, but I knew that I had only a few minutes left. I put both arms around her and kissed her for at least a full minute.

"Thanks for making my evening one of the most enjoyable that I have ever had," I said. "May I call on you again soon?"

"By all means. The sooner the better," she said as she opened the door.

As she walked toward the door of her house, I watched as she kept turning around to wave at me. As she was ready to enter her house, she blew a kiss at me. I could actually feel it touch my face.

That night, I went to bed overwhelmed with happiness. I could not think of anything but Mary Ann.

Monday morning, I went to school early. There were many friends that I wanted to see before classes began, as was our usual procedure every morning.

"Hey, Bobby Darrell, how was your date with Annette Funicello Saturday night?" quizzed Manny. "I sure would have loved to have been there to watch her slap your face a couple of times."

"I avoided all the violence that I could," I said. "I gave in to her charms and never made one move to give her cause for slapping me."

"The most common sounds at a Drive-In are: 'Stop that,' 'Do that again and I'll rip (something) out of you,' a slapping sound, 'Oh no, not again,' 'Take me home,' and, 'Bingo,' said Manny. "If you don't hear any of that stuff, you are not having any fun."

"Believe me! I had fun without all of that. I think that I have found my Peggy Sue. That girl may be a marriage prospect someday."

Charley was running quickly toward us. It was obvious that he had some good, or bad, news.

"Hey, guys, did you hear the rumor that Judy was pregnant? She said that the little one's last name will be White."

"There you go spreading rumors, Charley. If she is, it would be a virgin birth. You ought to know better than spread rumors about a girl being pregnant. That is the worst kind of rumor."

"You're right," said Manny. "I wouldn't want anyone to spread rumors that I was pregnant. It could ruin my reputation."

"What reputation? Now we are going to spread a rumor that you don't know anything about the facts of life and are concerned about getting pregnant. What would your classmates say about that?" asked Charley.

"Most would applaud me," said Manny.

"Or laugh at you," I said.

At first bell, I saw Diana and Roger walking into the building. She looked down and did not acknowledge me or anyone else.

Toward the end of the week, Mary Ann called me to pick her up Saturday and bring her to the Corlee for the afternoon. That meant that she would be with me for many hours. I told her that I would pick her up at 10:30 so that I could take her for a nice breakfast at the Three Point Grill, which was next to the Corlee.

"Oh, I can't wait. I am jumping with joy. Hurry up Saturday!" she said.

On Saturday, the Corlee was expecting a sell-out for the entire weekend. The movie "Thunder Road," starring Robert Mitchum was the main feature. The plot of the movie was about moonshine running in Harlan County, Kentucky. The movie was notable in that there was loud applause when Harlan County was mentioned by an actor in two of the scenes. I had a feeling that I was going to receive many requests from friends for free admission to the theater, which I did. But there were so many that I could not accommodate them all.

When Saturday finally arrived, I did my usual grooming for special dates. I hurried as quickly as I could so that I could get to Lynch and pick Mary Ann up on time.

As soon as I arrived at her house, she came running out of the door as fast as she could. She entered the car smiling and was excited to get started.

"I was looking out the window for you," she said. "I can't wait for the day's activities."

The Three Point Grill was busy as usual with the Saturday morning crowd. When we sat down at the table, Mary Ann looked around the restaurant. She seemed so happy. She was like a little girl in a toy store.

"What will you have?" asked the waitress.

"Ladies first, Mary Ann. Order what you wish," I said.

"I am not used to ordering. My mom or dad always orders for me in a restaurant. I will have the same as you."

I ordered eggs, country ham, homemade biscuits, and gravy. It was a hearty breakfast, but we both were hungry.

"This is good," she said.

"Eat well. This is the only meal, except for snacks that we can get at the

227

concession stand, until I get off at 6:00. I will then take you to dinner."

"To dinner? I have never been treated this well before by a date. It makes me feel like a queen."

"You ARE a queen to me," I said with a smile. And I really meant it.

After our breakfast, we went next door to the theater. A long line had formed and it was an hour away from show time.

"This is going to be big," I said. "The Corlee is going to make a lot of money today."

I picked up the film in the lobby that had been delivered that morning and opened the steel cases that they came in to inspect it. I checked to see if they were re-wound and ready for the projector. I loaded both projectors quickly so that I could have some extra free time to spend with Mary Ann.

"Let's go outside the projector booth and have a seat in the balcony," I said. "We can watch the movie from there.

We sat down and I placed my arm around her. She reached for my other hand and squeezed it.

"I am so happy to be here with you," she said. "I don't want this to end."

"I don't either," I said.

Chapter 22

"One should never do anything that one cannot talk about after dinner."
Oscar Wilde

After my shift ended, I treated Mary Ann to a nice dinner at the Big Top. I was tired from the day's work and activities, but she was as energetic as she was earlier that morning.

"I'll bet that you are anxious to go home," I said. "You seemed to enjoy your afternoon at the theater. We will have to do it again soon."

"I don't necessarily want to go home, but I will have to eventually," she said with a chuckle, "but all good things must come to an end, as they say."

"Everything that happened today was not good but excellent. I will miss you when you leave."

"When you take me home, will you spend some time with me on the front porch swing?"

"I thought that you would never ask. I will, indeed."

We sat on the front porch swing for hours talking. Now and then, she would look into my eyes and brush her lips against mine. She would then lightly kiss me in a teasing manner and giggle softly.

"What are your plans when you graduate from high school?" she asked.

"I plan to go to college at UKSEC, but I do not know where I will finish my education. I have no idea as to what my major is going to be. I have thought of careers in the medical, biological, or chemical field. But who knows what I will finally decide upon."

"I will also be attending UKSEC. At least we will be going to the same school for a while. I wish that you and I went to high school together. Would you consider moving to Lynch?" she asked with a laugh.

"That is as likely as you moving to Cumberland, isn't it? If you did, I would be the happiest person in the world."

"Do you plan to stay in the Tri-City area when you finish school?"

"I would love to if the opportunity presents itself. There are no well-paying jobs here except for coal mining and I am not equipped physically for that type of work, so I will no doubt have to leave Cumberland for a career that will fit my educational level and needs."

Mrs. Searcy peeked around the door and reminded Mary Ann that her curfew was approaching. I placed my left hand on her face, turned her head toward me and gave her a long, passionate kiss.

"Good night, my queen," I said jokingly. "See you soon."

"Not soon enough," she whispered.

Final exams for my sophomore year were near and I began spending a lot of time studying. I had to have the grades necessary to enroll in college; any extra free time that I could get was spent especially on the Chemistry and Biology courses.

On the day of the exams, I was ready for them. The first one was in Biology. The teacher passed the tests around and we waited with bated breath for the assigned time to begin. I looked around the classroom; a few students had a frown on their faces as they began to take the test.

When the teacher gave the word to begin, I went through the test rapidly. We had an hour to complete it, but I, and many others, finished it in about thirty minutes. I had the same experience with all of my other final exams.

At the end of the day, we gathered on the school grounds to say our goodbyes to some of our friends who we would not see until the beginning of the fall term. There were tears in many of their eyes as they turned and walked away.

"Let's go to the Big Top," Charley said. "After all of those exams, I could eat a couple of burgers and fries."

"May we go, too?" asked Judy, Patsy, and Marci.

"Hey, wait for me," yelled Manny.

The Big Top's parking lot was full and many others walked from school. We waited for a table to clear which took some time. I looked around the restaurant to see who else was there from CHS.

"Over there is your girlfriend," said Manny who was pointing in Leslie Goodman's direction.

"If she was my girlfriend, I wouldn't be standing here. I would have arrived with her."

"I also see Roger and Diana making goo-goo eyes at each other. I don't believe that they are looking at anyone else," said Manny.

"They make a nice couple. They have been together for quite a few months now. They are becoming a fixture around town. Roger is a lucky guy."

"I'll be right back. I need to see Miss Goodman."

"Hello, Miss Goodman. Are you relieved that school is finally over for the year."

"Not necessarily.   As I tell everyone in my classes on the first day, I love teaching. It is not only my job; it is my passion. What are you and your friends doing, terrorizing the town?" she asked with a chuckle.

"Yes, in a way. Want to join us?" I said jokingly.

As we talked, she was looking around the restaurant.   I knew that she was uncomfortable and watching for reactions to our conversation.   I took the hint that I should not tarry long.

"I just wanted to say hello.   It is always good to see you."

A table finally opened up for us after about twenty minutes.   The crowd was becoming so noisy that I could barely hear. We ordered our food which took some time to prepare and serve.   We wanted to get away from the noise as soon as we could, so we consumed it quickly.

"O.k., let's get out of here," I said. "Where do you all want to go?"

"How about Hoss' place in Virginia?" said Manny. "We haven't been there in some time."

"Who is Hoss?" asked Judy with a puzzled look.

"Just someone who owns a barn where you can drink, sleep, and listen to Bluegrass music," said Charley.

"Huh?" said Patsy.

"It is a private joke among us guys," I said.

"You guys are getting stranger all the tIme," said Judy. "Please speak slowly so that we can understand you the next time."

"We will save it for another day," I said.

We went to the top of Black Mountain, stopped at an overlook, exited the car, and marveled at the view, although we had seen it many times before.

"This is so beautiful," said Patsy as she moved close to me.

I placed my arm around her in a friendly gesture. Manny did the same with Marci and Charley held Judy closely.

"Every time I come to this spot, I am always awed at the sight of the peaks of other mountains that seem to never end," said Charley. "Viewing a photograph or painting could never compare to actually being at a site such as this."

"It is also romantic," said Manny.

"Romantic? You DO have a soft spot in that heart of yours," I said with a loud laugh. "There is still hope for you, Manny. Seriously, though you are right, Li Po's poem says it best":

All the birds have flown up and gone;
A lonely cloud floats leisurely by.
We never tire of looking at each other -
Only the mountain and I.

"That is so fitting. Words like that run chills up my back," said Judy. "I could stay here forever and look at that view."

"Me, too, but I have a few things to do. I also have to be at work at noon tomorrow. Maybe we can do this again soon."

When we arrived in Cumberland, I wanted to break away from the crowd. While I enjoyed the company of my friends, I occasionally wanted to either be alone or with only one person. I drove to the drug store and had a root beer float. The refreshing concoction awakened my senses and I became more aware of my surroundings.

Diana was sitting alone at the end of the counter with her head lowered. I looked around for Roger who did not appear to be in the drugstore. I was reluctant to speak to her; it was apparent that she did not hold me in high regard since she and Roger began dating.

"May I join you or are you here with someone?" I asked.

"No, I am not with anyone," she said. "I would enjoy some company."

"It appears that you are bothered by something very serious. Would you want to talk about it?"

"I am pregnant," she said.

"You are? How long have you known? Does Roger know?"

"I have known it for about a month. I just told Roger this afternoon and he broke up with me. He is not the father."

There would be no other questions from me, I thought. It would be wise to let her talk about it.

"We broke up briefly a couple of months ago, so I began my search for a new boyfriend. Billy and I started dating; one thing led to another and, to put it bluntly, he knocked me up. My mom and dad doesn't know it yet."

"The longer you wait, the angrier that your parents will be that you didn't let them know. I would tell them only if you know for sure, though."

"Would you see me occasionally? I need someone to talk to. I feel so alone."

"I will when I can. I have a girlfriend in Lynch now, and I do not want to jeopardize our relationship. If you need me, call me at the Corlee."

She looked at me with tears in her eyes. I had the greatest empathy for her, but there was very little that I could do except to make an attempt to comfort her when she needed it.

Chapter 23

"Ring out the old, ring in the new,
Ring, happy bells, across the snow:
The year is going, let him go;
Ring out the false, ring in the true."
Lord Alfred Tennyson

Now that I was a junior in high school, I had enough math instruction to take my dream course – Physics. I would finally get to study the basics of electricity, magnetism, sound, light, astronomy, and the structure and function of atoms.

The study of Physics required us to use slide rules; electronic calculators had not yet been invented, so some mathematical calculations took a lot of time and patience but I loved the challenge. We studied our Physics textbook for three days a week and spent two days in the Physics laboratory.

As soon as I received my Physics textbook (I still have that same book), I immediately began studying it. Within a few days, I had read and understood seven chapters and had taken the quizzes at the end of each chapter. I carried my book and slide rule with me wherever I went; I studied it in any free time I had to spare.

Our junior year in high school was also time for the undecided to discontinue their education upon graduation from high school or go on to college. In the year 1960, only 41.1% of the population completed high school, while only 7.7% graduated from college, so the statistics indicated that the number of our classmates who would pursue a college degree were minimal. My decision had already been made.

There was excitement among the majority of our classmates. At this point in our education, everyone who still remained in school would likely graduate from high school. There was hope and a feeling of accomplishment among us; we envisioned new beginnings once our diplomas were handed to us in just another year.

It was also at this time that I decided that I would resign my job at the Corlee Theater. I had been working there since the eighth grade and I felt that I should concentrate more on my studies. There was not much of a career as a projectionist, but it was something that could be added to my resume in a job search.

It was 1959 and near the end of another decade that came and went too quickly for me. I turned seventeen that year with a confidence that I could do anything. I was not the only person that felt that way, most of my classmates worked hard toward the attainment of their goals.

At the beginning of each new decade, the soothsayers are always busy with their latest predictions, and the beginning of the decade of 1960s was no exception. Many were predicting the end of the world at midnight on New Year's Eve, as they did at the end of every other decade, while others expounded the theory that the world's population explosion would result in mass starvation and death. Jetpacks, flying cars, and death rays, were other predictions that never materialized. I never worried about predictions of future events that did not have hard facts behind them, especially from those who were unqualified to make them.

On December 31, 1959, my friends and I celebrated New Year's Eve at Judy's house. I drove to Lynch and picked up Mary Ann who was all smiles as she entered the car.

"You don't know how much I have looked forward to this," she said. "This is the first New Year's party that I have ever been to."

"Really? I thought that a wild girl like you partied often," I said jokingly.

"Is that a hint that tonight's party is going to be a wild one?"

"With our group of friends, anything can happen."

Figure 17. Father Time and Baby New Year.

The Cassidy house was decorated throughout with New Year's paraphernalia including large likenesses of Baby New Year and Father Time. At the entry door, there was a poster with the words "All Who Do Not

Enter Here Are Squares," which was mimicking – in a way – the beginning of Dante's book "The Inferno," with the words "Abandon all hope — Ye Who Enter Here," which was Mrs. Cassidy's idea.

The neighbors must have been forewarned of the party; the music was loud and could be heard five houses down, and the house was brightly lit and could be seen at quite a distance. Doors were opened to all rooms that had them to discourage games that would lead to misbehavior among those whose hormones might become overactive in the celebration of the New Year's Eve.

Judy was dressed in a long gown that sparkled and a pair of shoes that resembled the ones that Judy Garland wore in "The Wizard of Oz." She also donned a tiara and carried a wand mimicking Glinda, the good witch of the North.

"That is a great costume," I said. "When the clock strikes 12:00 you will, no doubt, have a lot of wishes to grant."

"Yes, I will. I have many requests so far. What is your wish at midnight?"

245

"My wish would be that the 1960s will be as much fun as the 1950s. I hate to see the 50s end, but time must move on, I suppose. In 1961, we will graduate from high school and from that point on all of us must decide what we are going to do for the rest of our lives. I am looking forward to the 60s."

"Your wish is easy and will be granted at midnight," said Judy with a smile.

"Who is your friend?" asked Judy.

"Oh, I am sorry! I did not introduce her."

I introduced Mary Ann and she nodded her head toward the crowd in recognition of their welcoming comments.

As Mary Ann was conversing with her new-found friends, I had the time to break away for a few moments. I would rejoin her if she appeared to be bored or wanted my company.

"Judy, where is Manny and Charley?" I asked. "I have not seen them since I arrived."

"They are upstairs with a couple of girls from Benham. How they got them up there is another question."

"I would love to know what lies they told them to lure them away from the crowd," I said with a chuckle.

"Here comes Marci. She has been looking for you for some time. I will see you later. I don't think that I want to be around when the chairs start flying," quipped Judy.

"Hi, Bobby Darrell. Are you here with anyone?" she asked.

"Yes, were you not here when I introduced Mary Ann to the group?"

"No, I have been up and down the stairs many times looking for you, so I missed the introduction. Is she your new girlfriend?"

"Not exactly. We are currently dating, and that is about it. Why do you ask?"

"Why? Because I have asked you many times if you would spend more time with me, and you have never given me an answer. Am I not suitable to be your girlfriend?"

"Look, Marci, that question does not deserve an answer, so please drop it."

"What about your little tryst with Miss Goodman. I saw you leave with her one evening and bring her back very late. What were you two doing all of that time?"

I was now really concerned. What was I going to say to Marci to convince her that nothing took place between us? If she is telling others what she just told me, it would not be long before everyone would know our secret.

"How and where did you see us, Marci, and how would you know the length of time that I spent with her if, indeed, I did spend time with her?"

"You must pass my house every time that you see her. And I know exactly where you dropped her off. The color of that car of yours is easy to spot so it had to be you."

"I will not discuss it any further with you Marci, and I would be very careful with any gossip that you might spread. You would not only damage Miss Goodman's reputation; you would also damage your own without absolute proof of your allegations. It is possible that no one would trust you anymore with intimate details of their lives if you keep gossiping about Miss Goodman's. I hope that you have fun at tonight's party."

I could hear her sniffling as I turned and walked away from her. I was confident that she would say nothing further about Miss Goodman and me. She was hurt more that angered and I felt great empathy for her. She left the party as I walked toward Mary Ann's direction.

"Great party, isn't it, Mary Ann? Everyone is enjoying themselves," I said.

For the remainder of the evening couples danced, laughed, and ate some great snacks prepared by Mrs. Cassidy. Manny and Charley were the stars at the party. They imitated Elvis' dance from his movie "Jailhouse Rock" while demonstrating the Elvis sneer with the side of their lip. When Johnny Ray's recording of "Cry" was played, they pretended to cry and wiped their eyes on each other's shirtsleeve. Everyone was so amused at their antics that they kept asking for more.

The hours seemed more like minutes; it was 11:55 and everyone was preparing to leave shortly after midnight. At the top of the hour at midnight, the volume of the music was increased as Guy Lombardo's recording of the old Scottish folk song, "Auld Lang Syne," was played. We sang along with the music and gave the traditional kiss to our dates at its conclusion. We regretfully said goodbye to everyone; Mary Ann's curfew of 12:30 A.M. was getting close and I did not want to anger or worry her parents.

When we arrived at the Searcy house, I pulled off to the side of the road. The moment that I stopped, she began to sob.

"What's wrong, Mary Ann, is something bothering you?"

"These are not tears of sadness, but tears of joy. I loved the party and everyone there, although I did not know most of them. They treated me as their best friend and I appreciated that."

"You can always expect that from my friends. They are very special to me although they act a little nutty at times," I said with a smile.

"By the way, who was the girl that you were talking to at the party? She left just after your conversation with her."

"A friend who needed someone to comfort her."

"I must go, my mother turned on the porch light as a signal for me to come in. Kiss me like you have never kissed me before."

As I kissed her, she surprised me and placed my hand on her breast.

"The next time that we are alone, they are all yours," she said.

All mine? Now there was a thought that would remain with me constantly until I saw her again.

Chapter 24
"I wasn't really naked. I simply didn't have any clothes on."
Josephine Baker

In the month of May, 1960, I turned 17 years old. In August of that year, I began my senior year in high school, a memorable day that was cherished by not only me, but the entire graduating class of 1961.

It is difficult to describe my feelings on the first day of class as a senior with the exception of the feeling of accomplishment and the realization that this would end my many years of attendance in the Harlan County Public School System in Cumberland, Kentucky. I reflected on the years that I attended elementary school and I remembered fondly both the fun and the frustrations of a child who entered the first grade and was awed by the size of the elementary school, the teachers, the kids that I had never seen before, and the excitement of advancing to the higher grades. Becoming a senior seemed to take a lifetime but once that time had arrived, it would vanish seemingly in days.

As soon as I received my class ring, I looked at it for an extended period of time and marveled at its design. It was, to me, a symbol that represented a first step in the continuation of my education.

College would follow but education would not stop there. A college degree is merely a ticket that opens many doors of opportunity. Once you get through those doors, you discover that your education taught you a lot of theory but not the practical application of those theories. The practical side of one's education is usually learned in the workplace and is never ending as time and technology advances.

I joined the group of Charley, Manny, Johnny, Patsy, Judy, and Marci, who were discussing their senior year after the lunch hour. Spirits were high and the very thought of being a senior made most of them feel giddy.

"We finally made it," said Judy. "It seems so surreal that we are seniors. We all should celebrate by having another big party and bonfire at the old swimming hole. And let us make it a wild one."

"I am all for that if you will be my date, Judy," said Manny. "Since it is our last year in high school, you should at least let me fondle those treasures of yours a few times over the next few months."

"You wouldn't know how to if I would let you, Manny."

"I wouldn't object if you would want to teach me."

"You finally admitted it, you pervert! You don't know anything about a woman's treasures, as you call them. You keep boasting about your manhood but it is all fluff."

"If you will be my date at the party, I could show you my manhood. You might be surprised."

"I don't like anything small and inconsequential, Manny. You have no manhood to show."

"Hey guys, let's talk about the party," I said. "Who will we invite?"

"How about doing it the way we did the last time," said Patsy. "We will announce the party and invite everyone."

"O.k., spread the word," I said. "I hope that the crowd is a larger one this time."

The announcement got everyone's attention, and the excitement was growing. No invitations were sent – only word of mouth - so anyone could attend which added a little mystery as to who would be there. It was agreed that the party would be the following Saturday at dusk.

I wanted to invite Leslie Goodman but I knew that it would be inappropriate. I called her at home and asked if she could meet me somewhere at a discrete location. She agreed to meet me in the evening at a remote location that was about one-half the distance to the top of Black Mountain. I drove to where she directed me to which was out of the sight of traffic.

"I haven't seen you lately," she said as she entered my car. "I was hoping to see you sooner, but I understand that you have been busy with your school work. But you are here now, and that is all that matters."

"I have something to tell you that you are not going to like. Marci Canova said that she saw us come and go on the evening that we were in Gilly Holler. I did, of course, deny it, but she was accurate in the timing of it."

"Did she see my face?"

"It was too dark. I don't think so."

"Then I am not worried. If she could not see me, she wouldn't stand a chance of proving it. Why don't we concentrate on the present? I don't want to waste time on such trivial matters."

She moved to the center of the seat.

"I didn't really want to break the bad news to you. You seem to take it only lightly."

"I do take it lightly! You see, I am a person that doesn't worry over things that

COULD happen, only things WHEN they happen. If everyone worried about what COULD happen, can you imagine the state of a person's mental condition?"

"I understand! Then I will no longer worry about it. By the way, we are having a party at the swimming hole at Cloverlick this Saturday night. I am inviting you if you want to come."

"I think I will. I will come just to face Marci, if she is there, and get her reaction, but I will stay only a few minutes."

Wow, this woman is gutsy, I thought. Saturday night should be very interesting. I will be watching her and Marci very closely.

She reached for my hand and began stroking it. I put my arm around her and kissed her lightly.

"Is that all you got?" she said jokingly. "I want more than just a peck; I want the whole bushel."

She put her arms around me and gave me one of the longest and most passionate kisses than ever before.

"Let's go to the back seat. It is much nicer back there."

It was another unexpected night of bliss, which is better, I thought. Not knowing when, or what, her next move was going to be was exciting. I did not want our relationship to ever end.

"I hate to rush, but I must go," she said, as she quickly dressed. "My brother is visiting and he is waiting for me to go to dinner with him. We will get together again soon."

"Don't forget Saturday night. And thanks for another unforgettable evening."

"The feeling is mutual. I will see you then."

As Saturday approached, all that I could think of was the party at the swimming hole. There were many that confirmed that they would attend and the numbers increased daily. I invited some well-known local musicians that lived on Cloverlick that I knew to perform; they would play their signature country and bluegrass music with the proviso that I provide them with a case of cold Budweiser to chase shots of whiskey which they would provide. They assured me that the beer and whiskey would be consumed only by them.

I invited Mary Ann a week prior to the party, but her parents were a bit skittish about allowing her to attend a party with a number of people that she did not know, which I understood.

On Saturday, I drove to the party site just after 7:00 P.M. There were many cars that had already arrived and the crowd could be heard singing "Rocky Top" to the music of the band that started playing at 7:00 sharp. I unloaded a case of cold Budweiser for the musicians, and at the conclusion of "Rocky Top," which would be played multiple times before the party ended, each of them drank a can of their favorite refreshment.

"These musicians are good," said Charley. "They sound so professional. Where did you find these guys?"

"Actually, they live just up the road on Cloverlick. They have been playing together for many years. I think that all of them are related."

Now, the crowd was coming in ever increasing numbers. I was concerned that there would be too many for such a small area. Space was quickly becoming a premium and bodies were beginning to get closer as the numbers increased. I looked around the crowd and spotted many familiar faces including that of Leslie Goodman. She smiled as I approached her.

"This is some crowd," she said. "It looks like the party is going to be a big success."

"Too much of a success. I am beginning to worry about the number of people and they are still coming."

"I was looking for Marci. Have you seen her?"

"No, but I will continually look for her. Are you staying long?"

"I would love to, but I will have to wait and see what happens as the night proceeds. I love the music, by the way."

"Do you want to stay close to me, or would you prefer to mix with the crowd?"

"I will stay close to you. I already feel as though a thousand eyes are upon me."

"They are staring at you because you are beautiful; I would accept the compliment and mix with the crowd."

"Not tonight. I would prefer to play it safe."

The musicians started playing "Little Maggie" and the crowd started dancing and laughing at others who did not know any dance steps to bluegrass music. It was fun to watch them; Leslie started dancing in front of me.

"Come on and kick up those heels. I love this song," she said.

I made an attempt at it, but it did not matter how I danced. There were some who were worse than me, which made me feel somewhat better.

"Time for a dunking," said one the guests as he and his date dived into the water. "Come on in, the water is fine."

Within minutes, large numbers of guests dove into the water in their underwear and began screaming with delight.

"Time for me to leave," said Leslie. "I cannot be seen here any longer. See you soon."

"I understand," I said. "See you soon."

"Take them off," another guest yelled. "The last one to get naked is a wimp."

At his urging, the majority of those in the water took off their underwear and threw them to the creek bank. They playfully splashed each other and began dancing vigorously to the music. Manny became so excited that he joined the group.

"I want to slow dance with you when they play the next tune, Judy. All you have to do is take your clothes off and come on in and join me" said Manny.

"I have finally seen what you have and I am still not impressed," quipped Judy. "Maybe tonight in your wet dreams."

"You are cruel woman. When you finally realize what you are missing, I will treat you the same as you have treated me," said Manny with a loud laugh.

"I can take the punishment," said Judy.

Some began to exit the water, totally naked, and began searching for available private spots around the creek bank. They disappeared for twenty-five to thirty-minutes and then returned to search for their underwear.

"If only I had the nerve," I said to Judy. "I have to admit that it looks like a lot of fun."

"Come with me," she said, as she nudged me toward one of the private spots that had just been vacated. "We are going to have MORE fun than anyone here."

And we did!

"I didn't expect such a wild bunch," I said, as everyone started to leave at 11:00. "I am really embarrassed that things got out of hand. I am so relieved that Mary Ann was not here; it might have been the last time that I would have ever seen her."

"It is not your fault that things happened the way they did," said Judy. "By the way, did you enjoy our little lovemaking session?"

"You see the smile on my face, don't you?" I said.

Chapter 25

"The doer alone learneth."
Friedrich Nietzsche

On Monday morning, there was a lot of conversation about the party. Gossipers, who were not even there, were discussing the events as though they had participated in them. According to their versions, we were all drinking whisky, beer, smoking marijuana (known then as Mary Jane among us greasers), and raping all the girls. Questions arose among school officials as to what they could do to punish those who attended the "drunken orgy" of underage youth, and some churches condemned us all to burn in Hell for our evil ways, but hard evidence was lacking; all of the participants remained silent to the chagrin of their accusers. It was also concluded that school officials could not take any retributive action since the party was not school sponsored or held on school property.

Marci did not attend the party, but she was very vocal about it. We were all relieved when she was challenged by some of her close friends who threatened the end of their friendship with her if she continued to criticize them without knowing all of the facts.

The 1960-61 school year was, as Patsy Collins called it, the "ginchiest," a term borrowed from Ed "Kookie" Byrnes, a popular TV actor who appeared in the series "77 Sunset Strip." In addition to a trip to Washington, D.C. (which I did not take), we took a bus tour of a few colleges in Eastern and central Kentucky including, Berea College, Eastern Kentucky State Teacher's College (now known as Eastern Kentucky University), Centre College, and Union College. I did not attend any of the colleges that we visited; I would attend UKSEC and then Thomas More College, a private Catholic college, where I received my bachelor's degree in Accounting and Finance.

Graduation day was fast approaching. We received a small folder with "My Senior Year" embossed on the cover with pre-cut slots for attaching name cards from each of our classmates and space for recording information about our high school and commencement.

On the evening of Tuesday, May 23, 1961, ninety-five of our classmates participated in the commencement exercises. Our class motto was "Anything worth doing is worth doing right or not at all," words that I lived by all of my life, although not obtained from that motto.

As I sat through the commencement exercises, I looked into the faces of proud parents beaming with pride at their sons and daughters who were about to receive their high school diplomas. I

Figure 18. A proud graduate of CHS.

knew that a large number of those in the audience never completed high school; some had no more than a fourth grade education, but they encouraged their offspring to complete their education so that their lives would improve over their own.

After receiving our diplomas and the "turning of the tassel" from the right to the left side of the mortarboard, the crowd responded with applause and the yells of parents to their proud graduates. I could not wait to go outside into the fresh air after commencement to meet with my family and friends.

"I don't know about you, but I feel a lot smarter since receiving my diploma. I feel like the scarecrow in 'The Wizard of Oz' who didn't have a brain until he was awarded a diploma by Oz. Man, he never even went to school to get his diploma; he got off easy," said Manny.

"Yeah, me too," said Charley. "I do feel smarter, so my next move is to find a job, but there is nothing around here but coal mines. I don't think that I would want to work at any of them."

"I want to go on to college," I said. "I don't know what field that I want to major in, but I will find out after a year or so."

"I am not college material," said Manny. "I am thinking of starting my own

269

auto repair business. There are more and more cars on the road, so it looks like a great future."

"I have to run, guys, I don't want to keep my mom and dad waiting," I said. "I will see you around soon."

After twelve years of education, I felt that obtaining my high school diploma was the most important step toward what success that I would have later on in life. I went home, a short distance from CHS, sat on the couch and contemplated my future. Where would I go after college? What would I do? How, and when will I meet success? What are my goals?

Those were just a few questions that I asked myself as I inadvertently drifted off into a restful sleep.

Life can be such a mystery. But living it is a joy.

CPSIA information can be obtained at www.ICGtesting.com
Printed in the USA
LVOW10s0217130715

445983LV00001B/21/P

9 781502 361134